MW00574188

BUILDING A

KILLER
TEAM

Published by Inspire and AVAIL

For foreign and subsidiary rights, contact the author

Cover design by Bogdan Matei

ISBN: *978-1-957369-11-2*   1 2 3 4 5 6 7 8 9 10

Printed in the United States of America

BUILDING A

KILLER TEAM

WITHOUT KILLING YOURSELF OR YOUR TEAM

SHAWN LOVEJOY

AVAIL

INSPIRE

CONTENTS

INTRODUCTION

am proud to say I have raised three amazing kids. They all love God, love each other, and love their parents. The older they get, the closer we all become. Being their boss for years has allowed me to become their buddy at this stage in their lives. Make no mistake; parenting has been one of the most difficult leadership responsibilities I have ever undertaken. Raising three kids has exposed every root sin and every leadership flaw I ever had! Parenting has also served as a great parallel to my efforts in building a killer team at work.

If you are a parent, you will quickly relate. You love your children like no one else, but there are still those moments, especially while your kids are still living at home, when they just . . . well . . . grate on your nerves! They've been doing something all week that just gets under your skin. You didn't say anything about it at first, but the longer it goes on, all you know is that you want them to stop—and stop now! However, you're either too tired, too busy, or too frustrated to take the time to explain why.

You simply turn and say, "Would you just stop it?!"

It never fails, and it's disrespectful. You get the "w" word in return: "Why?" This, of course, generates that response that you vowed never to use when you grew up: "Because I said so."

- Raise your hand if you know that parent, or you've *been* that parent.
- Raise your hand if you have been that leader to your team. You know, the leader that is too distracted, busy, and fatigued to really communicate.
- Raise your hand if, just like me, you have expected behaviors from your team but failed to slow down long enough to define those behaviors or give the reasons behind them.
- Raise your hand if you have tolerated less than desirable behaviors for too long on your team.
- Raise your hand if you have been unclear with your team, developed a short fuse with members of your team, or made team members walk on eggshells around you.

What do we really expect from the team we lead anyway? Better behavior? A greater ability to play well with others? More self-awareness? Stronger people skills? Heightened ability to read a room? Higher capacity to manage emotions? More flexibility? Increased ownership? Better execution? Faster pace? More consistency?

The answer is, "Yes! We want all of those things!" And we're not wrong for expecting them. The right leader always wants more from their team and more for their team. This is the reason you picked up this book. Deep down, you already know that.

> The right leader always wants more from their team and more for their team.

The right leader doesn't just build a staff. A staff is corporate. It's institutional. A staff is a human resource tool used to get the work done. But it's more than that. Leaders build people. They use the work to get people done, not the other way around. Leaders need to view people not just as scaffolds they climb on their way to the top but as the brick and mortar that they're building with. Your and every leader's greatest legacy will not be the logo attached to your organization. Your greatest legacy will be the people you build.

Building a platform, wealth, and a monument to yourself is so empty. Your work will become the most fun—and the most fulfilling—when you focus on building people. After years of leading and coaching in both ministry and marketplace sectors, I've finally embraced this fundamental truth: we are all in the people business. The sooner you realize it, the happier you will be. People are not the problem or the distraction from your work. They are your work. They are the goal. Building a killer team is our greatest calling and will be our greatest legacy.

> Building a killer team is our greatest calling and will be our greatest legacy.

Without people, our work is useless. You will not get very far without a killer team. The book you hold in your hands will help you build that team. I promise. Stay tuned!

Your friend and coach,
Shawn Lovejoy

CHAPTER

1

MY CONFESSIONS (AND YOURS)

have been a real estate developer, church planter, mega-church pastor, leadership coach, and founder and CEO of a fast-growing coaching organization. I have been building and leading teams since I was twenty-three years old. Wow, I just realized that.

Confession: I am an expert at building a killer team . . . by failing a lot. As I reflect on the teams I have led over the last twenty-plus years, I don't have too many regrets. The regrets I do have, however, center around people and relationships. There were times as a young leader when I did the right thing the wrong way and hurt people. Or, I was so exhausted that I developed a short fuse with those around me.

There have been times I've been too busy to invest in my team the way they needed to be. I have managed rather than led, or I didn't care for my team the way they needed to be cared for. I have used people to get the work done.

There were times I tried to protect my team to a fault and shouldered too much of the responsibility. I didn't utilize my team the way I should have to help me solve complex issues that were really over my head. Wow, did that cost me!

I have micromanaged. I have hired and fired wrongly. I've chosen to be popular instead of respected, and it ended up costing me the privilege of being liked. I waited too long to have that courageous conversation with a teammate or friend in too many instances.

This cost us all more than it should. I have lost friends in the process of trying to change the world. So, why should you even listen to me? The most encouraging news of this book is that leadership can be learned. I got better, I improved, and I learned. I hired coaches and sought perspective. I read, I worked at it, I prayed about it, I journaled, I practiced, and I grew. I made progress and began to experience the fruits of my labor as I built a killer team. I began to teach all that I had learned and coach leadership teams around the principles contained herein. What you hold in your hands is the culmination of thousands of hours of coaching and training sessions with leaders. I have taught these principles from Nigeria to Ukraine and from New York to Hawaii.

> Build people: a team
> made up of human beings,
> not just human do-ings.

You can grow, improve, and become a better leader. You, too, can learn how to build. Building *something* is not enough. Build people: a team made up of human beings, not just human do-ings. Build a team. No, that's not enough. I want you to build a killer team. Actually, that's not enough, either. I want you to build a killer team without killing yourself or your team!

Merriam-Webster defines the word "killer" in two ways. First, as a noun: "One that kills." That seems obvious, but it also sounds fairly ominous, so let's avoid it. I want you to build a killer team, but I don't want you to kill yourself in the process. I also don't want you to kill your team in the process of building whatever it is you feel called to build.

DEFINITION

KILLER
A) "ONE WHO KILLS"

B) "**STRIKINGLY IMPRESSIVE OR EFFECTIVE**"

SOURCE: MERRIAM-WEBSTER

The second definition for "killer" is an adjective: "Strikingly impressive or effective." I love that definition. It encompasses so much of what I want for your team. This leads us to the book you're holding in your hand, and you need to know one thing from the outset: This book is about the adjective. It's ultimately about putting the killer in your killer team. Teaching you how to build a strikingly impressive and effective team.

I didn't say it would be easy. If it were easy, everyone would be doing it. They are not. Another thing is for sure: You won't build a killer team overnight. The best leaders are formed in the Crock-Pot, not the microwave.

> The best leaders are formed in the Crock-Pot, not the microwave.

All that's required to build a killer team without killing yourself or your team is a plan and commitment. I call this plan the Killer Teams Framework. The book you're holding contains all the elements of this framework.

I am now the author of four books, but honestly, I've never written a book. Every book I've authored has boiled up out of our coaching. I coach. I write it down. I repeat. So here is a fair warning for you grammarians out there: this book will not fit into a grammatical book style. And, as it's not intended to be a book but a coaching conversation, I will write as though you and I are having one.

By the way, a book is a great way to initiate change, but it won't be enough. Every breakthrough leader has had a coach. Every breakthrough team has had a coach. Therefore, I believe every leader needs a coach! We would love to be your coach. I hope you don't even finish the book before we have a conversation about that. At Courage to Lead, we would love to help you through the pushback, speed bumps, hiccups, and setbacks to make sure you don't give up on building a killer team. In the meantime, however, I will give you almost everything I know on teams in the work in the book you now hold in your hands. Stay tuned!

At the same time, the faster you begin putting the lessons you learn into practice, the faster your frustration will recede, and the faster your team will generate momentum. I am honored you picked up this resource, and I am honored to be your coach along the way. I am so pumped about helping you build your "strikingly impressive" team! This is my confession and declaration, and it needs to be yours. Let's do this together.

CHAPTER
2

THE DISTINCTIONS AND PILLARS OF A KILLER TEAM

THE DISTINCTIONS AND PILLARS OF A KILLER TEAM | 23

M ay I confess something else? I don't just come right out and say this very often either, but I need to begin our journey with total transparency.

But first, let me share an idea statement with you that is honestly so simple it's profound: A staff doesn't make a team, but it can become one. I have made that statement a lot in my lifetime: keynote speeches, blog posts, podcasts, interviews, coaching sessions, and the list goes on and on.

A staff doesn't make a team, but it can become one.

I have coached team-building for over twenty years, and I have highlighted the fact that there is a difference between a staff and a team almost every single time . . . which leads me to my next confession. When I expose the difference between a staff and a team, almost every leader I speak with agrees with me, but few of them really do anything about it. This simple fact gets me up every morning. My head pops up off the pillow with holy discontent, slightly frustrated that leaders out there are killing themselves and their teams.

What does it take for a team to become a killer team? How does a killer team differ from the average team? There's a difference between the average staff in an organization and a killer team. In this chapter, I want to give you a small handful of ways you can recognize the difference.

So, what does it take for a team to become a killer team?

How does a killer team differ from the average team?

1) THE AVERAGE STAFF FOLLOWS BECAUSE THEY MUST. KILLER TEAMS HAVE A LEADER WORTH FOLLOWING.

As leaders, we have big visions, strong ideas, and—let's admit it—strong preferences and opinions! We are also hard-charging our goals.

We're running fast, and, if we were all completely honest, we might admit that we find it difficult to slow down long enough to really be a team player.

Leader, may I be your coach for a minute? You want to build a killer team? It begins with you. Killer teams follow killer leaders. Start by understanding that effective leadership requires slowing down long enough to take people along with you. It takes time to communicate and explain the details. Then, we have to slow down to listen to feedback and allow leaders to weigh in, so they will truly buy in.

We need to get better at team. We need to care for people more effectively and refine our ability to work with people, so we steward people more effectively.

We could make the call without consulting the team. We could save ourselves the hassle and fly solo. Many "successful" leaders also tend to be difficult to work with. I would even include myself in that description sometimes!

We need to get better at team. We need to care for people more effectively. We need to refine our ability to work with people. We need to steward people more effectively.

In the long run, our success will largely rise and fall based on the health and quality of our team. We need a team—a killer team—if we want to fulfill our potential.

2) AVERAGE STAFF MEMBERS DON'T REALLY TRUST EACH OTHER. KILLER TEAMS MAINTAIN A HIGH LEVEL OF TRUST.

Stephen Covey wrote a fantastic book called The Speed of Trust. He essentially says that when trust is high, speed is high, and cost is low. When trust is low, speed is slow, and cost is high.

Take communication for example. In a high-trust environment, you may say the wrong thing, but people may still understand what you mean or give you the benefit of the doubt. In a low-trust environment, you could be very intentional in what you say and yet may still be misinterpreted.[1]

Jesus was the greatest leader who has ever lived. He embodied "grace and truth." He addressed issues with both mercy and kindness, honesty and truth. When you follow His model, you build trust with those on your team. Lingering issues and artificial harmony are venom to your leadership. Quickly resolve issues with honesty and kindness.

When leading people, there are times when we do not like everything that happens. Here is a principle you can hang onto: send problems up and praise down. Fighting for trust is handing an issue up to leadership and reserving positive things to pass down to those under you. If problems are handed down instead of up, you are not fighting for trust; you are proving yourself unworthy of trust.

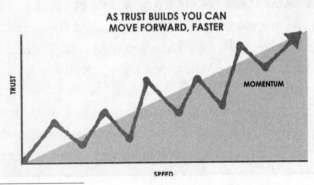

1 Kevin Lloyd, et al., "4 Differences between Unhealthy and Healthy Churches," *OutreachMagazine*, 17 July 2017, https://outreachmagazine.com/features/17222-4-differences-between-healthy-and-unhealthy-churches.html.

3) THE AVERAGE STAFF MAINTAINS ARTIFICIAL HARMONY. A KILLER TEAM PURSUES HEALTHY CONFLICT.

Too few leaders realize the value and power of saying the last 10 percent—they're comfortable with the first 90 percent, though. I like to call it "fighting for trust." In any situation, the healthiest way to discovery is by way of courageous honesty. As potentially painful as it is to be transparent, it is more painful to discover someone has been harboring ill feelings for a period of time.

So many teams are plagued by artificial harmony because they don't practice transparency and truth-telling. Living in the tension of telling the truth facilitates authenticity and health, and truly listening to those closest to us gives us our best opportunity to grow.

As a leader, we should always push our team for that last 10 percent. That's where the gold is! It gets us into what people are really thinking, how they feel, and gives us our best opportunity to gain rapport with those closest to us.

However, people are people. Defensiveness and insecurity run rampant among leadership teams. Don't get me wrong, most teams have a deep desire to grow and get better, but for some reason, they have a hard time listening to feedback, critiques, and heartfelt honesty.

Your job is to facilitate honesty among your team, keep it at the forefront and normalize what it means to share the last 10 percent. While honesty is not natural for many, your job as the leader is to make honesty normal for everyone on your team.

4) THE AVERAGE STAFF SAYS EXCELLENCE IS A VALUE. A KILLER TEAM TURNS EXCELLENCE INTO A HABIT.

Everyone should strive to do their best work. Excellence should be a value that guides your work, drives you to deliver more than is asked, and pushes you to constantly improve.

However, excellence has a dark side. Unguarded excellence creates unrealistic standards of perfection.

Perfection is a singular, elusive moment. Excellence is not an act, but a habit.

While everyone strives to do their best work, they are not shackled by the false god of perfection. In his book *Moving Past Perfect*, Thomas Greenspon referred to the following anonymous quote:

> *Excellence is risk. Perfection is fear. Excellence is effort. Perfection is anger and frustration. Excellence is openness to being wrong. Perfection is having to be right. Excellence is spontaneity. Perfection is control. Excellence is flow. Perfection is pressure. Excellence is confidence. Perfection is doubt. Excellence is journey. Perfection is destination. Excellence is acceptance.*

Perfection is judgment. Excellence is encouraging.
Perfection is criticizing.[2]

Healthy teams fight the monster of perfect outcomes by reframing an elusive value into consistent habits. For example, creating an organizational habit of returning calls or emails within twenty-four hours is a value that is easy to hold others accountable to that creates a culture of professionalism. Making excellence a habit frees a killer team up to be more fulfilled and effective and less stressed than the pursuit of perfection ever could.

5) THE AVERAGE STAFF REVOLVES AROUND THE SMARTEST PERSON IN THE ROOM. KILLER TEAMS HARNESS THE BRILLIANCE OF EVERYONE IN THE ROOM.

Leaders of healthy teams have a good handle on their ego. While they may have a solution to a problem, they know their job is to draw the best solution out of their team. Oftentimes, this means the best leaders are also the quietest team members. They know their words trump the room, so they hold them for strategic moments, allowing the best results to come through the giftedness of others.

You may be on or leading an unhealthy team. Your team may feel far from "killer." There's hope. Tenaciously

---

2 Thomas S. Greenspon, *Moving Past Perfect: How Perfectionism May Be Holding Back Your Kids (and You!) and What You Can Do about It* (Minneapolis, MN: Free Spirit, 2012).

practicing good habits, clear communication, and defining realistic expectations can help move a team towards health. Don't give up. Health is worth fighting for, so go fight for it!

Healthy things grow.

Healthy teams thrive.

Healthy teams are killer teams!

Health is not easy. The gravitational pull downward is strong. Teams have to fight to get healthy and stay healthy. My own team fights daily to maintain a healthy culture.

I have learned that the differences between a healthy team and an unhealthy team can be subtle. What appears healthy on the outside may harbor conditions robbing teams of effectiveness. Charting the course from an unhealthy team to a healthy, high-performing killer team is something this book equips you for and provides the framework to do so.

I'm not all that old. As I mentioned in the last chapter, I have now been formally coaching leaders for over twenty years. Maybe I haven't seen it all, but I've seen most of it. I've learned (often the hard way) of all the tensions that you're going to face. I've observed literally hundreds and hundreds of organizations in the for-profit and nonprofit worlds, the marketplace, and the ministry.

I can say with absolute confidence that I can trace every tension and opportunity in your organization back to one of three areas: the culture, the team, or the systems. You've probably heard all of these subjects talked about online or read multiple books on the subject. Ironically, however, as I looked around, there weren't as many resources as I would have guessed that spoke practically and at length about the greatest of those tensions. At Courage to Lead, we talk about coaching leaders through what keeps them awake at night. Once again, with confidence, I can tell you that the number one thing that will keep you awake at night is *people*. Leading real people with real personality profiles, Enneagram numbers, and love languages is one of the most difficult endeavors you will ever take on.

> Leading real people with real personality profiles, Enneagram numbers, and love languages is one of the most difficult endeavors you will ever take on.

If God blesses your work, you are going to need to build a team. That team will be made up of real people from very different family backgrounds, faith stories, political persuasions, races, and socio-economic levels. Your apprehensions, struggles, questions, frustrations, doubts, and mistakes are going to center around those you have the opportunity to lead in your organization. What I want to do is really zero in on this "Team Tension" and how anyone can build a killer team without killing yourself and your team.

THE KILLER TEAMS FRAMEWORK

There are five critical steps you will need to begin to get your head and your heart around. I can promise you in advance, if you will follow and weave these five steps into your life and leadership, you can build a killer team without killing yourself or your team.

The 5 Pillars of a Killer Team

1) Fostering togetherness
2) Recruiting (and keeping) the best talent
3) Bolstering accountability
4) Structuring for growth . . . and peace
5) Maintaining rhythms and finish lines

STEPS TO BUILD A KILLER TEAM

1. TOGETHERNESS
2. TALENT
3. ACCOUNTABILITY
4. STRUCTURE
5. RHYTHM + FINISH LINES

CHAPTER
3
FOSTERING TOGETHERNESS

T he first and most critical step for a leader is to take all of the assembled talent (the best you've got for now) and get them to want to be together and work *together*. No, it's more. They should *foster* togetherness.

How do we get there? First of all, someone has got to take responsibility. That's going to be you. Jim Clifton, in *It's the Manager*, cites research that reveals only 22 percent of workers strongly agree with the statement that the "leadership of their organization has a clear direction for the organization."[3] So, here's the first lesson. You may have not been as clear as you think you've been.

Often, when I am sitting across the table or desk from a client, I use this example. I don't do dairy, so when it comes to milk, mine never comes from a cow. I reach for soy or almond milk. (Don't knock it 'til you try it!) If I open the

---

3 Jim Clifton and James K. Harter, *It's the Manager: Moving fro Boss to Coach* (New York: Gallup Press, 2020).

fridge at home and grab the soy milk carton and empty its contents into my cup, the old Shawn would say to my wife (who's a stay-at-home mom and has grocery duty), "Tricia, can you get me some soy milk? I'm out!" What I assume Tricia heard in that moment is that I want her to grab soy milk at the grocery store *today*. When I open the refrigerator tomorrow morning, I plan on it being there for my coffee or cereal.

If that doesn't happen, I'm frustrated, and I make my frustrations known. Did I tell my wife I expected the soy milk to appear in our fridge in less than twenty-four hours? I did not. I expect her (men, you understand this) to read my mind and know what I'm thinking. I expect her to measure up to my mental (perfect) expectations . . . to fill in the gaps.

In reality, who's fault is it that the soy milk didn't get purchased before the next morning? Mine. I never expressed the expectation I had in my head either verbally, or even better, in documented form. Even if I had yelled from the fridge my expectation of having my blessed soy milk by the next morning, I didn't specify the *brand* of soy milk I wanted. Frankly, I have no idea whether my wife was listening (perhaps not) or if her schedule even allowed for the possibility of executing my request. Lesson one: I have usually not been as clear as I think. Now, I am frustrated, and my wife is agitated. Lesson?

What is lesson two? Most people tensions are systems tensions in disguise. The solution for our soy milk (and other grocery items) dilemma? There's an app for that. If someone in our home wants something on the grocery list, they must add it to the virtual "grocery" list we created in the cloud. Everyone in our family has access to it, and everyone now knows that Tricia goes to the grocery store on Tuesdays. If we want something from the grocery store, it must be placed on the list before then. This one simple system virtually eliminated all grocery tension on the Lovejoy team!

Good systems can do the same for your team. That's why, in the pages to follow, you won't just find content. You will find a system. If you will run the play, you can and will build a killer team without killing yourself or your team.

> Most people tensions are systems tensions in disguise.

You must get clearer about your expectations. You must get clearer about the vision. You've got to get clearer about your strategy. You have to clear away the clutter. People today are looking for meaningful and fulfilling work, and you've got to provide it. It's not just what you're doing; it's why you do it. Remember: Build people—not just a monument to yourself. Your greatest legacy will not be that thing you build; it will be the people you build in the process. Your job is to maximize the potential of the people you have around you and the team you have now; then, build on that. How do you build a killer team without killing your team? You build people. You help the people around you feel like they are experiencing real growth and development under your leadership.

Patrick Lencioni, in his book *The Advantage*, says the competitive advantage in any organization is a highly talented, highly cohesive leadership team.[4] So, here's your call to action: today as we begin on this journey together, I want you to schedule intentional, consistent meetings on your calendar with all of your direct reports. How many people are reporting to you? We're going to talk about structure in a later chapter, but for now, I just want you to level the playing field. Have a weekly meeting with everyone that directly reports to you, one-on-one. Then, once every week (or at least every other week) collectively meet as a team. I'm going to teach you how to meet with them, and how to structure that time effectively and more creatively a little later. But for now, I want you to just get it on the calendar:

---

4 Patrick Lencioni, *The Advantage: Why Organizational Health Trumps Everything Else in Business* (San Francisco: Jossey-Bass, 2012).

schedule weekly one-to-one meetings with each of your direct reports. Why? Because at the end of the day, your success will ultimately be determined by the team you are able to build.

Leading a team is like raising a family. Tricia and I have three kids. As the kids have grown up, sharing a family meal around the table on a consistent basis has always been a challenge! Everyone is busy. Everyone has their own task lists and agendas. It's like air traffic control to get everyone at the table at the same time to share a simple meal together. Many times, it requires pushing through the excuses and the drama and virtually threatening everyone to get them to the table. Then, without fail, after we have all sat for a while and enjoyed the time together, someone will inevitably say, "We need to do this more often." Why?! Are you kidding me?

See, one of my roles as a leader is to help each person discover and embrace the value of sharing life, doing life together, and discovering the strength we have together. My role as the leader of the team is to foster togetherness. I need to champion it, establish it, and share the value of it. I need to hold people accountable for getting to the table. So it is with your family, and frankly, any other team you will ever lead. And when you foster togetherness, you lead the multiple parts to discover and embrace the value of being together and working together to accomplish something bigger than what any one person could do alone.

At the forefront of fostering togetherness is the dreaded "m" word: meetings. Meetings must transition from something that's avoided and endured to the centerpiece of everything we do. To make that happen, we must embrace the fact that everything that's good happens in a meeting: decisions, innovation, leadership formation, personal development, strategy, and execution.

THE FOUNDATION OF A KILLER TEAM

Two thousand years ago, a small team came together to change the world, and it accomplished that very purpose. In the first century, they were called followers of The Way. Today, we call that movement Christianity.

Acts 2 records the components of the team that literally changed the world: "They devoted themselves to the apostles' teaching and to fellowship, to the breaking of bread and to prayer. . . . All the believers were together and had everything in common."[5] History tells us that this killer team had three things going for them.

---

5 Acts 2:42-44 (NIV).

MUTUAL DEVOTION

The founders of Christianity weren't just devoted to the mission. They were devoted to each other! They were committed to *fellowship*: a very unique, even intimate bond with each other. They were 100 percent unified. The Bible tells us they were in "one accord," and that doesn't mean they rode in a Honda together! The New Living Translation describes it as having "everything in common." What's interesting about these statements is that, on the surface, they didn't have everything in common. They were all so different, but the common vision they had for their mission united them. They realized that the strength of their relationships with each other determined the velocity of their mission.

Every killer team understands the same principle. We must be committed to the vision and to each other. We don't want to just do our job. We don't want to just accomplish the mission. We want to do it *together*. Great teams are mutually devoted: they are committed to both the mission and each other.

> Great teams are mutually devoted: they are committed to both the mission and each other.

PROXIMITY

A staff doesn't make a team, but it can become one. For that to happen, we must spend time together. We must rub elbows. We must circle the wagons. We must *really* get to know each other. We must build trust. We must learn each other's strengths and weaknesses. We must sharpen our communication skills. We must learn how to play well with others. We must hold one another accountable. All of this flows out of our commitment to spend time together!

As we endeavor to do that, we simply must spend time together. We're going to have to fight for it. It won't be easy. It's like getting everyone to the family dinner table at the same time. It's a real challenge. It's a calendar nightmare! Trust me; I will help you build that great environment once you get there. For now, just make the commitment.

CONSISTENCY

One of a leader's toughest tasks as a leader of an organization is to train their team members to see what they see and think how they think. Because this only comes with lots of time spent together, you must be consistent in meeting with your team. Here's the biggest question: What do you do when you get to the table together? Stick with me.

Most of us dread meetings because we have been exposed to a meeting structure that is out of balance. For

meetings to maintain a healthy culture, they must fulfill
five basic purposes:

- Community
- Communication
- Collaboration
- Coaching
- Cheering each other on

These five components of meetings must be woven into
the very fabric and frequency of your meetings. In the pages
that follow, I will unpack each one.

CHAPTER

— 4 —

THE FIVE PURPOSES OF MEETINGS

Stop having meetings that don't matter. A wasted meeting is wasted time which is our team's most precious commodity. If we convene, it must matter. However, this doesn't mean we throw the baby out with the bathwater. We must meet . . . consistently!

If you don't want the passion to leak out of your organization, if you don't want silos to form in your organization, or if you don't want your high-capacity players to be frustrated, have meetings . . . that matter!

I want to help you with this. Now, I've never led a bad meeting if you know what I mean (okay, maybe a few). I have not always been as prepared as I needed to be. I have apologized for that. You should as well. I have indeed led a few bad meetings.

As a leader and coach, I've been *a part* of many bad meetings as well. I have witnessed some very bad examples. I have also witnessed some of the best. So, in case you have a friend who's led a bad meeting . . . there's help! I want to help you with this.

COMMUNITY

Remember I said that leading a team is like raising a family. It's one thing to tell my kids I love them, but all parents know what communicates love to our kids more than anything else: consistent quality time. If I tell them I love them, but I'm always too busy for them, my actions contradict my words. Nothing communicates love to my family more than spending consistent time with them. So it is with every team you will ever lead.

I have a fundamental question for you: Why do you meet with your team? To strategize? To get stuff done? To hold them accountable? Sure, all of these are important, but they are not the main reason to meet with a team. Why do we meet with our team? Because we care about them. We desire spending time with them. A killer team leader never says to his/her team: "Hey, do we really have anything we need to talk about, or can we just skip this meeting?"

Do you see what a leader does with that kind of statement? They communicate that the only reason I want to spend time with the team is when there is a problem to solve, a decision to be made, or something that has to be done. As long as you are staying out of trouble and hitting your numbers, I don't value being with you. I don't realize it, but I have in a sense created a transactional relationship. I don't want to meet with you unless I need something from you. You are a human *do-ing,* not a human *being.*

Why do we meet together? Because we care about each other. Because we value each other. Because we want to know what's going on in each team member's life. Because we want to invest in and develop each other, and make each other better!

> Why do we meet together?
> Because we care about and value
> each other.

COMMUNICATION

Many of the frustrations and tensions in an organization can be traced back to poor communication. We're going to have to fight this every day. We must provide time and space to make sure everyone knows what's going on. The left hand must know what the right hand is doing. I need to help each team member learn to care about what's going on among the other areas of the team. I need to make sure everyone knows how they fit into the big picture. I need to make sure everyone understands clearly what their roles and responsibilities are. And all of this happens best in the context of our meeting rhythms.

On killer teams, effective communication is practiced. Every participant in a meeting should come to the table with at least three of what I call "just so you know"s. In pop-corn-like fashion, I want us to pop around and quickly share three things that we are working on, or we think everyone could benefit by knowing. The truth is most people on the team don't even know what other members of the team do on a weekly basis! As the leader of the team, I just want you to update me on what you're working on, what's going on in your area. You and I might even know, but everyone else on the team probably doesn't know—or care—and we need to help them care!

It's intriguing to learn how every task and team member fits together, to know what your team members do on a daily or weekly basis. The "just so you know" time is my opportunity as a team member to make people care about and value my area of involvement in the organization. It is my opportunity to help everyone value my role on the team and my role in the organization. Opting out of this portion of meeting by saying something like, "I don't really have anything to share," is not an option. This is my shot to inject influence and passion into the meeting, so I am prepared to share about what I am working on in every meeting I attend.

Yes, this includes the leader of the team! The truth is that they don't know what I do with my time either, so I am looking to offer them a glimpse into my world as the CEO. I also never want to surprise my team, so I'm going to communicate first face to face. All of this makes my team feel so much more of a part of my world . . . and it makes me feel part of theirs, as well! Let's fight to communicate!

COLLABORATION

Leaders won't buy in unless they weigh in. So, I'm always also looking for opportunities to tackle strategic issues with my team. Instead of feeling like I have to solve them on my own, I invite my team to be part of the process. You need to work for some places, spaces, and meetings where you invite members of your team to speak into strategic issues.

> Leaders won't buy in unless they weigh in.

I love leading with a statement like: "Guys, I have been thinking about something, but I would love to hear your feedback." I can literally feel the body language in the room change. Everyone looks up. People scoot up in their chairs. They lean in. My observation? Most people don't need a big title, large paycheck, or bonus to feel important. They just want to feel valued in the decision-making. They desire to have a voice. They don't even have to make the decision. They just desire to be a bigger part of the process.

COACHING

In coaching conversations with C-suite leaders, I am sometimes asked: "When should I address an issue with a team member?" When do you confront issues on the team? The sooner the better, the smaller the better. My observation is that coaching leaders through smaller issues normalizes the relationship when bigger issues need to be addressed. One of our tasks as a leader is to normalize coaching conversations among the team.

> When do you confront issues on the team? The sooner the better, the smaller the better.

When do you address an issue with a team member? Every day, every week, every month. There's great opportunity to bring this conversation into our normal meeting rhythms to make coaching a more routine part of what we do and how we develop people. I'm going to talk at length later about how to more consistently develop your team and how to approach those conversations, but for now, focus on stretching the muscle in this week's meeting.

Just say something like: "Hey, guys, glad you are all here today. I noticed we are about seven minutes late getting started because of a few stray sheep we had to wrangle into the meeting today. When we are late to a meeting, we may not realize it, but we are unconsciously communicating that we believe our schedule to be more important than everyone else's. Let's set a good example to each other and show we don't take other people's schedules for granted by being seated and ready to go for our meeting at the appointed time. Is that a deal for next week's meeting?"

Notice I didn't use a hammer to swat a fly. Sixty seconds of coaching could make a lot of difference. As the leader, when I am preparing for a meeting, I am literally thinking about vision, values, behaviors, culture, etc., and how I can coach my team to close the gap this week between what we say we value and how we really behave. Much more on this subject later, as well!

CHEERING EACH OTHER ON

Truett Cathy, the founder of Chick-fil-A, once said, "No one ever died from too much encouragement." There's a reason why that company has dominated the fast-food market over the last thirty years, and it has less to do with chicken than we might think!

Here's a question you have never been asked. Why do you think someone decided to put cheerleaders on the sidelines of an athletic field during competition? Because in every game, the players get tired. In every season, they inevitably get down. Every player has those moments when they want to give up on a game. That's where cheerleaders come in! They rouse the crowd. They get it back into the game. They pump enthusiasm into the stands. They keep everyone pumped up! As the leader of the team, that's our job as well. No one wants to be managed, but everyone wants to be inspired. If you will make encouragement and inspiration part of your meeting rhythm, your meetings will become the highlight of your team's week.

> No one wants to be managed, but everyone wants to be inspired.

Every job has its difficult aspects, . Every job has its downsides. Every year has its bad weeks. Every team member faces tough days in their personal and professional lives. Every team member has days when they wonder if they are making a difference. Every person has days when they think about quitting or joining the transfer portal. In fact, some experts are calling 2021 the year of "The Great Resignation." Abhinav Chugh, of the World Economic Forum, explains:

> *The Great Resignation is an idea proposed by Professor Anthony Klotz of Texas A&M University that predicts a large number of people leaving their jobs after the COVID pandemic ends and life returns to "normal."*[6]

At any given time, upwards of 50 percent of all employees are strongly considering changing jobs or quitting altogether. How do we keep that from happening on our team? We help them get taped up after injury, get them back into the game, and cheer them on to victory!

One final note about encouragement. I warn leaders about being a "politician encourager." I think you immediately know what I mean. You've seen a politician encourage the crowd. With thumbs up, while they are backing away

---

6 Abhinav Chugh, "What Is the 'Great Resignation?' an Expert Explains," *World Economic Forum*, 29 Nov. 2021, https://www.weforum.org/agenda/2021/11/what-is-the-great-resignation-and-what-can-we-learn-from-it/.

or ducking into the car, they shout abruptly, "Appreciate you guys; you're the best," and then they leave town. How does that type of encouragement come across? Less than genuine? Less than authentic? Less than sincere? You bet.

Killer team leaders are specific in their encouragement. They call names. They outline specific behavior in their encouragement. They encourage privately, as well as publicly. Look for opportunities to single out specific people on your team for a job well done, for values lived out, for exemplary behavior, for closing a big deal, for knocking it out of the park. Tell stories, specifically, to hearten your team members and spur them on toward love and good deeds. Make your encouragement count.

Try this. Pick up your smartphone right now. Think of one admirable trait, behavior, or job well done by a person on your team. Shoot them a quick text that says something like this: "Tom, just wanted to shoot you a quick note to thanks for the way you (trait or recent activity). I don't say it enough, but I'm honored to have you on our team." You don't have to be the President of the United States; Tom might still take a bullet for you!

Meetings with Meat on the Bones

Our family has three dogs. From time to time, we surprise them with a bone. Sure, they will take it, but they love it even more when there's a little meat on the bone! Picture your meetings as the bone. Sure, everyone will take them because they have no other choice. However, to build real anticipation and enthusiasm, put some meat on the bones of your meetings!

Begin with community. Start with relationships. Ask about everyone's weekend. Talk sports or shopping. Reveal a little from your life. Talk about your vacations coming up. What will you do for the holiday? Smile. Laugh. Then get down to business. Communicate. Collaborate. Coach. Then, end by specifically cheering on a couple people on your team and tell a story about how and why the vision is happening because of them. If you will follow this simple recipe, get ready. You have all the ingredients together to build a killer team, and you'll be able to do so without killing yourself or your team!

NAILING YOUR VALUES AND BUILDING TRUST

NAILING DOWN YOUR VALUES

As a coach, I am a huge fan of building and maintaining a set of team values. These are values that outline behaviors and how we treat each other as a team. They become a "code," or covenant that documents our behaviors in how we treat and relate to each other. They bond and unite us. They help to foster togetherness! If vision is the *why* and strategy is the *what*, values are the *how*. They determine how we behave while we do what it is we do.

As I stated earlier, Clifton's research suggests only 22 percent of team members believe the leadership of their organization has a clear direction. You cannot allow this to be your story. If you want a competitive advantage in today's marketplace it begins with greater clarity around what your team is all about. Ironically, however, perhaps the most common mistake I see leaders make is lack of clarity around its vision and values. Your job as the leader is to make sure your values are behaviors that can be measured, coached, and reviewed. Begin with clarity and end with accountability.

> Your job as the leader is to make sure your values are behaviors that can be measured, coached, and reviewed.

The first thing you need to know when it comes to nailing down the core values of your team is that there is a difference between aspirational values and actual values. True core values are mostly things we already value. We may or may not have made a documented list, but there are already things we value on the team. These are the things that we already tend to talk about a lot. These are the subjects we have in mind when we are interviewing a potential hire, and they frustrate us when they are missing or violated.

For example, few things bother me more than being late. If I am late to an event or meeting, and you haven't heard from me, you can assume I am on my way to the hospital or the morgue. That's how serious I am about being on time. Guess what frustrates me most often in the team environment? When someone else runs late for my meeting. See, whether I have communicated it to my team or not, being on time is a core value for me.

You want to know something else that really frustrates me? When someone says they will get back to me and then they never do. They are unresponsive to my text, phone call, or email. They may fail to follow through, or they simply don't do what they said they would do! So, two of our core values on the Courage to Lead team are responsiveness and follow-through.

This is *our* final list. This should not be *your* list. If the stated values don't boil up out of your bones, your core values will not be your core values! So, begin to make a mental list. Ask yourself these questions:

What are the things we actually already value around here?

- What do we celebrate?
- What frustrates us?
- What is often a determining factor in who we hire and who we fire?
- What occupies us based on the discussions that we have?
- These are your actual values.

COURAGE TO LEAD
VALUES

We are Healthy

We model the way, practice what we preach, and understand that success is being loved and respected by those closest to you.

We Follow Through

We do what we say we will do. We start on time and end of time!

We are Honest

We practice integrity. We share the last 10% of what we're thinking.

We are Responsive

We promptly respond to our calls, emails and texts. We maintain the 24-hour rule.

We are Polished

We maintain professionalism in all aspects of life. We prepare for meetings and come ready to add value to you and your company or ministry.

There are some things that you value that aren't currently happening on your team. Maybe you value being on time, but currently no one on your team runs on time! Maybe you value loyalty among teammates, but lately gossiping and backbiting run rampant among. This means that promptness and honesty are more aspirational than actual values right now. The point in the exercise is to outline both a list of actual values—things that already exist among the team—and a list of aspirational values—things that you may not value right now, but you'd like to.

Add to your list of actual values some aspirational ones. Together, these should be boiled down to a list of between four to seven principles or behaviors that become your core. Keep in mind, this doesn't contain everything you value. You are not trying to put too many things on your list because you can't scale what your team can't remember. Keep it short and simple.

These values should also be measurable, coachable behaviors. For example, I am not a fan of "excellence." I can't measure that, and I don't know what it looks like. "Resourcefulness: doing the best we can with what we have been given," is an example of a clearer behavior that allows for better accountability. If built properly, this list of core values becomes part of your regular team training, coaching conversations, performance and development reviews, hiring and orientation processes, and more. You can download the "Building Your Core Values" worksheet over at killerteambook.com.

Nailing Down Our Core Values

Actual :: **3 - 5**
(How we behave now)

Aspirational :: **3 - 5**
(How we want to behave)

-
-
-
-
-

-
-
-
-
-

Final Core Values
(3 - 4 Actual & 1 - 2 Aspirational)

-
-
-
-
-

> You can't scale what your team can't remember. Keep it short and simple.

EARNING (OR RE-EARNING) TRUST ON YOUR TEAM

Have you ever heard a team member say, "Why can't everyone just leave me alone and trust me to do my job?" (Perhaps you've even thought this yourself.) Whoever asked this question does not understand trust. Trust is something we earn, build, and work to maintain. It must be held in high regard. Trust is also something that can be broken, violated.

As I said earlier, leading a team is like leading a family. I've raised two teenage daughters that are nearly grown now, so consider this scenario with me, and apply it to your team. Imagine you're the dad, and one of your daughters comes into the den and says, "Hey, Dad, I'm going out with this guy. I don't think you've met him. I'm not sure where we're going or what time we'll be back, but I just need you to trust me." How does that hit you? Do you trust your daughter now more than you did five minutes ago? Nope.

However, if one of them comes to me and says, "Hey, Dad, I'm going out with Nick. You've met him. He goes to _____ church [I'm liking him better already]. We're going down to Sonic to grab a Sonic Blast, and I'll be home by 11 p.m." When 10:59 p.m. comes that night and in walks my daughter, trust is built. Then, weekend after weekend, my daughter continues to be where she's supposed to be and comes home when she's supposed to come home. Do I trust my daughter more or less at this moment? You got it. More. Why? High levels of communication followed by high levels of consistency have allowed her to earn my trust. So it is with your team.

Trust is something you can build in a relationship and earn on a team. How? Through high levels of proactive communication and consistency as evidenced by your track record over time. By the way, this starts at the top. I shouldn't ask my team to "Just trust me," either. As the leader, I need to be a trustworthy person. Trust is built three-hundred-sixty degrees through and moves at the speed of the communication and consistency of our team.

The more proactive each of us can be in our communication and the more consistent each of us becomes, the more we will earn each other's trust. The more details we give about what we're working on, whom we're working with, and how our division fits in with the whole, the more trust we will earn. The more we do what we say we're going to do when we say we're going to do it, the more trust we will earn.

When one of my team members says something like: "Hey, Shawn, just so you know, this _____ (potential problem) popped up. I'm on top of it. I reached out to _____ (so and so). I think it's handled, but I will keep you posted and let you know if I think you need to get involved," why, that's music to my ears! If you are a second- or third-chair leader, the best way to help *your* leader with their micromanaging tendency is to be more proactive in your communication. The more "in the know" I am as a leader, the less I tend to micromanage. On the flip side, if knowing what's going on in your area of the team is like pulling information out of a hostile witness on the witness stand, then I just don't trust you so much. Trust is a two-way street, and we must meet each other there.

Once we have communicated at a high level, my track record of performance matches my walk with my talk. If I do what I say I'm going to do over and over and over, I'm going to earn high levels of trust on my team. Let's just say, hypothetically, you realize you've blown it when it comes to properly maintaining the trust level with your team. (You at least have a friend who's done this, right?) Can you re-earn your team's trust? Well, here's the greatest news: If trust is indeed something we build and earn and something that can be broken, this also means it can be rebuilt, re-earned, and mended!

> If trust is indeed something we build and earn and something that can be broken, this also means it can be rebuilt, re-earned, and mended!

Two of the most credibility-building words a leader can say is, "I'm sorry." Your team already knows you've blown it. They just want to know if you have the emotional intelligence to recognize it and the humility to acknowledge it! When you do, everyone is like, "Whew! He finally admitted it!" They are ready to forgive. But wait. You will need to establish a new track record . . . be willing to be held accountable . . . take the responsibility to communicate at an even higher level in the short run. But with high levels of communication and high levels of consistency over time, you can and will re-earn your team's trust.

Put this into action this week. Open the meeting by saying, "Hey, guys, I owe you all an apology. I have dropped the ball some lately when it comes to _____ (behavior or value you want to provide to your team). I want to set a good example and model our values, and I just haven't done an effective job lately. I'm sorry, and I am giving you all permission to hold me accountable." Guess what just happened in the room. The trust meter just moved up.

BUILDING A LAST-10-PERCENT TEAM

I'm about to make an accusation against your team: Most of you are liars. You are not completely honest with each other. You hold back, don't say what you are really thinking. When you leave the meeting, you will tell someone else how you really feel. You will go home to your spouse and complain about this person or that person . . . without having ever shared that frustration with the "guilty" person.

I can't tell you how many times I have sat across the table from a leader and listened to them as they went on for twenty minutes to tell me how frustrated they are with a person for whatever reason: behavioral problems, performance issues, or just lots of small things that are getting on everyone's nerves. After what usually tends to be a long discourse from them, I respond with this penetrating question: "Have you ever told them what you just told me?"

"Well, no, not exactly like that."

Ah, the honesty gap. The honesty gap is the gap between what we think or say to another person and what we are willing to say to someone's face.

What is it that keeps us from saying what's really on our mind? Simple answer? Fear. We are afraid: of rocking the boat . . . of making things weird or awkward . . . of losing a relationship . . . of not being liked . . . of losing our job. We are afraid! One of my life verses from the New Testament says: "For God has not given us a spirit of fear, but of power and of love and of a sound mind."[7] If fear doesn't come from God, where does it come from? The evil one. The devil. The one who comes to steal, kill, and destroy you and your team by getting you to talk *about* each other rather than *to* each other.

I can hear you. "Okay, Shawn, what's the big deal about being less than completely honest with each other?" Make

---

7 2 Timothy 1:7 (NKJV)

no mistake, it's a very, very big deal. Why do most organizations eventually stop growing? They choose not to have the courageous conversations that are necessary in order to make the courageous decisions they need to make. It takes courage to have those conversations, confront tensions, behavioral, and performance issues on the team, and confront the elephant (or the person) in the room. It takes courage to lead!

WHAT WE OWE OUR TEAM

It's easy to think about what they owe us, but what do we owe them? If you are the leader of a team today, there are three fundamental things you owe your team: grace, honesty, and proper placement. Let me explain.

Grace

First of all, we owe our team grace. We offer patience and forgiveness while we help people make progress and let them know we don't expect perfection. Let your team know that it's okay to make a mistake now and again as long as we don't keep making the same ones.

Honesty

Second, we owe honesty to each member of our team. When I say honesty, I mean real gut-level honesty. If we are frustrated by and thinking about moving someone on your team because that person's not meeting your expectations, or you're thinking about releasing someone, and they would be surprised by that conversation, then you haven't been completely honest with them along the way.

Most people say about 90 percent of what they're thinking and hold back the last 10. I believe the strength and health of a team comes from getting that last 10 percent on the table. This means that everyone present makes the commitment to share their last 10 percent. By the way, the last 10 percent belongs inside the meeting—not outside of it—and in this order: we dialogue, we debate, we decide, we commit, we have each other's backs. Period.

> On a killer team we speak to each other, not about each other.

I have actually made this radical promise to my team over the years: "I promise never to go home and say something to my spouse about you that I'm not willing to say to you." You might want to read that again. If you think about it, saying one thing to a person's face and another to someone else, lacks integrity. Integrity in the context of a killer team means we speak *to* each other, not *about* each other.

It only makes sense, then, that if that's what I am going to extend to you, then that's what I expect *from* you. This may cause some uneasiness from time to time in our meetings. Our relationship could get uncomfortable. We may actually have more conflict at first, but the opposite of conflict is not peace. It's artificial harmony. Harmony is great. Artificial harmony is not. With artificial harmony, we smile and nod our head but . . . we don't *really* think it's a good idea. We don't *really* agree. We aren't *really* committed, and we don't *really* have each other's backs.

Killer teams don't have artificial harmony. Why? They experience healthy conflict. Healthy conflict avoids sarcastic jabs, making it personal, shouting, and making threats. If you've committed any of these, you need to apologize. As you've been reading this, maybe you have been convicted. Someone has come to your mind that you need to speak with. Maybe it's the entire team! Just walk into your next meeting and open by saying something like this:

"Hey, guys, I owe you an apology. I have not always been completely honest with you. I have held back my 10 percent—at least in this room. Then I have inadvertently shared what I really thought with another person. That's not right, and it keeps us from having the depth of dialogue I want us to have in our meetings and the type of relationship

I want to have with each of you. Today is a new day. I am committed to stretching my courage muscles and being more upfront with each of you. That means things might get awkward at times between us. I might need to choose to be respected over being popular at times. We will probably have more conflict, but at least we'll have integrity in our relationship, understand each other better, make better decisions, and trust each other more. So can I count on you to make this same decision with me?"

Stretch the muscle. Have a courageous conversation this week. Many leaders and teams are just one courageous conversation away from new momentum in their organization. I'm so excited for you. You are about to build a killer team.

Proper Placement

I am about to make a controversial statement. I am not a big fan of personality, strengths-based assessments. The honest truth is that I don't feel like most of us are great assessors of our own talent. Remember the early episodes each season of *American Idol*? Suzy had traveled from Iowa to Los Angeles to audition. The show gave her story before she even auditioned. She was a beautiful, sweet girl who'd been sleeping in her car for days to get this opportunity. We couldn't wait to hear her sing . . . until she finally did! Turns out Suzy was completely tone-deaf. She couldn't carry a tune in a bucket! The entire time she was singing, however, we found ourselves thinking, *Where is Suzy's mother? Couldn't she love her enough to tell her and save her this public humiliation in front of millions of people?* Enter Simon Cowell. He told her. He crushed her. Someone had to tell her because, evidently, she was not a great assessor of her own talent. Sadly, she is not the only one. Most of us need an outside perspective to truly assess our strengths and our weaknesses. We don't know what we're really good at until we have performed in front of others.

As the leader on a team, one of the best gifts we can offer our team members is to honestly assess and communicate a team member's strengths and weaknesses from our perspective. "Hey, Tom, you're really good at _____(strength) but probably not as gifted as you think in _____ (weak spot)."

Raise your hand if you are honest enough to admit that you have potential "blind spots" in your leadership. Blind spots are quirks or flaws of which we are unaware. Raise your hand if you know what your blind spots are. Don't raise your hand! If you know what they are, they aren't blind spots anymore. You still have some, however. You will need someone else to help you identify them and root them out. Your team members will need the same from you.

Every team member deserves to be in a place on the team that matches their skill set and capacity. The worst thing we can do for a team member is keep them in a seat on the bus that places them over their heads and outside their giftedness. This causes personal and professional tension. To put it frankly, it causes a team member to feel unsuccessful. We owe every team member the privilege of being in the right seat on the bus. The best thing we can do for someone is be honest with them about their strengths as well as their weaknesses, and what we see (or don't see) as potential places in the organization in their future. The sooner and more consistent we have this conversation, the better.

6

RECRUITING (AND KEEPING) YOUR BEST TALENT

R emember, one more person won't solve your problems because every new person is a potential problem!
We don't just want more people on the team. We want
the right people on the team. You are not just building a
team. You are building a killer team. You need elite talent
with killer speed and killer instincts. Elite talent must be
recruited.

> We don't just want more
> people on the team. We want the
> right people on the team.

I love college athletics. Specifically, I'm a very big college
football and basketball fan. If you're not, that's okay, but

you need to understand this: The best college coaches are great recruiters. Yes, they understand the Xs and the Os. However, elite coaches know that the right Jills and Joes can beat anyone's Xs and Os. See, the right strategy, process, or product isn't enough.

If you want to be elite, you must surround yourself with elite talent. Great coaches are all great recruiters. The question is how, right?

Average talent will make a YouTube reel (resume) with killer music (full color) and killer snapshots (references from friends), and send it to every coach (company or church) they can. They basically self-recruit and self-select.

The best talent, killer talent, always has to be recruited. They don't need to send a highlight reel. Their track record speaks for itself. In fact, they really aren't even looking to be recruited. They love it where they are and are crushing it already. We actually will need to help them see what they are missing out on and give them a compelling reason to consider leaving where they are. We will need to work to get noticed. To stand out from the other teams. We will need to help them understand the value of joining our team.

At the top levels of my organization, I'm not looking for people who are actively looking for a job. I'm looking for people that are crushing it somewhere else or, even better, someone who has their head down and is crushing it some-where *within* our own organization.

This is yet another reason why I must have enough margin in my day-to-day leadership to rise above the grind long enough to look around, dig, and make a few recruiting visits down the halls, across the street, and across the country. It's great to have five-star earners. But people graduate (retire), move, and leave. People's life stations change, their spouse gets transferred, etc. So, if you put all of your eggs in one basket, so to speak, and everything rises and falls based upon the temperament, the personality, and the talent of one person, it makes your team fragile, volatile. Championship one season, and can't win a game the next.

Build a deeper bench. You need to build a next-man-up/woman-up mentality. If one person leaves and everything goes to hell in a handbasket, then I haven't done what I needed to as a leader in building a deeper bench and developing the talent pool. This is true not just for me, but all of my coaches (my top leaders) need to be elite recruiters, as well. They need to get out of the office more. They need to be developers, not just doers.

One common mistake I see leaders make when an organization is growing rapidly is only hiring technicians for their executive team. They hire doers for leadership roles. We hire people that have a specialized skill, but they don't know how to reproduce themselves in others. They don't play well with others. They are great at some very specific things, but they're not recruiters and developers of talent.

Therefore, when that person (and that person could be one of us) steps away from the team, it creates a huge vacuum. Let me encourage you. Everyone on your team must focus on recruiting and developing talent. Everyone needs to understand the importance of building teams and raising up leaders at every level. We must hold every leader on the team accountable for reproducing themselves. If you don't have an internship program, start one. If you don't offer systematized leadership training, start it. If you have never hired a coach, do it. Let's get busy building a killer team by recruiting and developing killer talent.

OBJECTIVELY ASSESSING YOUR TEAM

I promised you would learn how to build a killer team without killing your team. And one of the best ways you can do that is by learning how to more objectively assess your current and future team. Ready? Great. You've probably heard some derivative of this. There are basically four filters for who gets and stays on a killer team: character, chemistry, capacity, and calling.

Character

According to a study released by the Washington, DC-based training company, Leadership IQ, 46 percent of newly hired employees will fail within the first eighteen months in a new job.[8] Only 19 percent achieve long-term success with that team. Contrary to popular opinion, however, technical skills are not the primary reason why most new hires fail. Instead, about 25 to 30 percent of new hires fail because they can't accept feedback, they're unable to understand and manage their emotions, and they lack the necessary motivation to excel. Lesson? Character and humility matter. Teachability, coachability, and self-control matter. And, healthy psyches and emotions and integrity (in the small things) matter.

Here's a test. Schedule lunch or coffee off-site in the middle of an interview. On the way to the parking lot together, ask the potential hire if they mind driving. You can learn so much of what you want to learn by observing how the candidate handles traffic and traffic laws. Are they easily aggravated, ? Are they frantic? Are they oblivious? Do they observe traffic laws? Will they run through a yellow light? Do they use sign language in their communication with other drivers (and you know what I mean)? We want leaders to have character.

---

8 Jana Gregorio, "Skills vs. Attitude: What Drives 89% of Hiring Failures?" *Recruiting News Network*, 3 Aug. 2021, https://www.recruitingnewsnetwork.com/posts/skills-vs-attitude-what-drives-89-of-hiring-failures.

Capacity

I have a good friend who is CEO of an executive search firm who told me the number one question you must ask yourself before you hire someone is: "How long do you I expect them to be in this position?" In other words, how fast and how large can the organization grow and this person excel in this the position you're hiring them for? If we hire them and then outgrow their capacity after our organization grows by 50 percent, we may need to slow down and think about this.

These are the capacity questions: Can this person scale with us? Can this person keep up? Can this person lead us to the next level? Does this person have a high ceiling and experience? Have they ever led a team at an organization of this size? Can this person build teams and raise up new leaders? Can this person delegate? Can this person move around in the organization because their skills are transferable, or is this seat on the bus their only viable option? Do they have the capacity to lead beyond where we are now? Can they lead sitting in the same seat to as well as one that is three times the size it is now?

I heard John C. Maxwell, *New York Times* best-selling author and speaker, but also former pastor, say this years ago at a conference: "The reason why most churches in America aren't growing is because they have ushers that can't ush, and no one will tell them!" In other words, churches have leaders in positions that those leaders aren't qualified to serve in, and no one will confront that elephant. It happens in churches and it happens in companies, too—people occupy positions on the organizational chart for which they are not gifted and qualified to fill. If we don't address this, it will affect our momentum over the long haul.

Interestingly enough, it was Dan Reiland, former executive pastor for John Maxwell and one of the founders of John's leadership company INJOY, who told me this years ago. If you've been rocking along with a team member with little or no tension for a long time, then suddenly, during a rapid growth season, you feel new tension with that team member, it's the number one sign that this team member has hit their capacity lid.

Many of the teams we worked with during the COVID-19 pandemic had at least one team member go a little crazy on them during the pandemic. There was new tension, drama with a team member that ultimately became toxic to the team. Sometimes the team member had to be released, and sometimes they simply pulled the ripcord themselves and left in a rapid, unhealthy fashion. What happened? Did the pandemic cause this? No. The pandemic simply exposed an issue—a capacity issue. Pressure crushes rocks and forms diamonds. Be careful not to hire someone your organization will outgrow too quickly. This is the capacity filter.

> Be careful not to hire someone your organization will outgrow too quickly.

Chemistry

In Jim Collins's book *Good to Great*,[9] he found no difference in the amount of "churn" (turnover within a period of time) between the good-to-great and the comparison companies. But he did find differences in the pattern of churn. People either stayed on the bus for a long time or got off the bus in a hurry. In other words, the good-to-great companies did not churn more; they churned better. Their unique vision and culture quickly spotted and selected or helped leaders self-select when they didn't fit the culture of the company.

In our coaching with organizations over the years, we have had many fast-growing companies and even churches reach out to us because they felt like the culture had gotten unhealthy in the midst of rapid growth. Why and how does this happen? I speak about this at length in my book *Be*

---

9 Jim Collins, *Good to Great: Why Some Companies Make the Leap...And Others Don't* (New York: Harper Business, 2011), Kindle.

Mean About the Vision,[10] but basically a fast-growing organization is hiring lots of new people, many of them because of their specialized technical or competency skills. They have experience with another organization that maintained an entirely different culture.

Hiring someone based on technical skill and experience and failing to spend the proper time with them to "indoctrinate" them into your culture is asking for trouble. A team member must not only possess the competence for the organization, they must also be willing to maintain the company culture you want to maintain and align with your organization's vision. This is vision chemistry. When interviewing a potential candidate, you must spend time not only assessing their proficiency but also explaining and allowing them to experience your culture. Doing so on the front end could save you a lot of pain.

Years ago, I was interviewing a high-level hire for the team I was leading at the time. After spending the entire day experiencing all of our normal meetings, the prospective team member called me the next day to say: "Hey, I don't think I am a fit for your team. You lead a very collaborative team that has lots and lots of meetings. I am actually introverted, and I tend to like to work alone and be left alone a lot."

---

10 Shawn Lovejoy, *Be Mean About the Vision* (Nashville: Thomas Nelson, 206) 8, Kindle.

I said, "Thank you very much. You are right. You would hate working here."

When is the best time to get divorced? Before you get married. The same is true for your team. The time to fire someone is before you hire them.

Chemistry is ultimately all about fit. Does this person fit with me, my team, and our culture? First of all, if I am developing my team correctly, I'm going to be spending a lot of time in meetings with those who report to me. I don't need to just love my team. I need to like them. I need relational chemistry with each person. I need to enjoy spending time with them. Our personalities can't clash. We can't rub each other the wrong way all the time. We can't get on each other's nerves easily.

I like to envision myself sitting at my desk or working in my office and looking up to see a team member standing at the door. At that moment, will I be really glad to see them? Or is it like, *Oh no, what do they want?* Sometimes the wrong fit is not about character or capacity. It's just chemistry. It's like oil and water. Both are alright independently and serve their purposes. They just don't mix all that well. Sometimes, there's a member of on the team that just does not blend. No one's right or wrong. It's just not a fit. Everyone knows it and will wonder if you notice it and are willing to address it.

Calling

This fourth filter may not be as familiar to you. When I talk about "calling," as a filter for who gets selected and who stays on the team, I'm talking about a team member's willingness to pay the price. Many people want the privilege of being part of a killer team, without paying the price of being on a killer team. It's easier to work alone. It's easier to be left alone, and not be sharpened. It's easier to punch in, punch out, and go home every day at 4:30 p.m., leave Friday afternoon and not think about the organization until Monday. It's easy if you match my salary and 401(k) and give me cushy benefits and lengthy maternity and paternity leaves.

The problem with all of this is that being part of a killer team requires sacrifice and treating this as more than a job. People will never just "leave me alone." It may require a short-term financial sacrifice, long hours, or long weekends. Killer teams are made up of people with killer instincts. They are driven, self-starting, self-motivated. They are called to build something, well . . . killer. Because they are called, they are naturally willing to be the first one there and the last one to leave, to turn on the lights or turn them off. They care more about the goal than the role, whatever that looks like.

One of my coaches, Sam Chand, told me years ago that there are only two types of leaders. Person one: The type of person that you virtually have to kick them in the seat of the pants (virtually, not actually kick them, even though you might be tempted) to get them to move along at the desired pace. They love people, they love coffee, and they love standing around and talking to people while they drink a lot of coffee. They move at a snail's pace and don't get much done without us goading them about it. Person two: This type of person might make a mess now and again, but you only have to steer, coach, and correct—you never have to drive them. You actually need to pull this person back and restrain them from time to time, make them shut down for the day, or actually take a real vacation. You have to tell them not to text you at 9:00 p.m. just because they are still working.

The good news? You get to choose what type of person you recruit to your team. Person one or person two. My observation is that it's possible to coach lots of team members to greater health and rhythms, help them learn how to shut down at the same time every day, and hold them accountable to taking a vacation and not email us while they are there. I have been able to teach high-octane team members how to better get along with their team members and not blow everyone out of the water and create a bloodbath in their wake while they are changing the world. On the flip side, I have never been able to place a *drive* in someone. I have never been able to motivate someone that wasn't self-motivated. I have never been able to coach *pace*. Guess which one I have chosen. You must choose, as well.

You have probably heard or read some derivative of the four Cs, but there is the big mistake I see leaders make. Too many leaders, when assessing current or potential team members, overemphasize one C at the expense of another. The candidate is brilliant, but he/she is not teachable and coachable. They have great people skills, but we noticed they exaggerated things a few times during the interview process. If you overemphasize skill at the expense of character or character at the expense of skill, it will eventually cost you.

As you seek to objectively assess a potential or current team member (let's call him "Tom"), you'll need a simple way to do that. You are assessing Tom's ability to go to the next level with you. To do this, we're going to create a simple, small scorecard. Write the candidate's name at the top. Then, below score Tom in each of the four categories on a scale of one to ten.

TOM
CHARACTER (1-10): __7__
CHEMISTRY (1-10): __6__
CAPACITY (1-10): __6__
CALLING (1-10): 7
TOTAL: 26

Note: I'm never going to share this tool or score with Tom! This is for my private, personal use. In the exercise above, Tom received a comprehensive score of twenty-six. Now I can compare Tom with other candidates for the same position or the next level. By the way, we provide this simple, downloadable resource for you at killerteambook.com.

DETERMINING WHO STAYS ON YOUR TEAM

Many people will come and go over the years. Most people will not stay on your team for the long haul. Your goal is not to hang on to every team member forever, but to hold them loosely. They don't belong to you; they belong to God. He simply entrusts them to your care for a season. You want to be a good steward (manager) that wisely manages God's prized assets: people.

However, there is one major benefit of being the leader of a team. It is rarely talked about. It's the benefit of determining who stays on your team. If you are the leader, you should have the right to not only hire, but also fire team members. Even if you don't have this privilege, you can make things so painfully clear for them that they self-select and opt-out. You should be consistently evaluating, not only the types of leaders you need to join the team, but also determining who's going to make it with you to the next level. You've got to determine who stays and at this level and gets the opportunity to climb with you to the next.

CHAPTER

7

DEVELOPING YOUR TEAM

t's one thing to recruit talent to your team. It's another thing to develop them to another level altogether once they reach your team. Your job as a leader is to love your team members enough to refuse to allow them to get too comfortable. You want to squeeze every ounce of potential out of them. Especially if you're one of those leaders in one of those organizations that, by the very nature of resources, you have to pay on the lower scale of things, your great advantage is your ability to invest in and develop your team. In today's world, people are quitting jobs that pay more and are accepting less to be in a growth environment. It's not worth it to be paid more but left to grind it out on their own. How do we build a leadership development culture on our team?

CARE

When it comes to retaining your best talent, caring is more powerful than money. One of the reasons I am not a fan of having too many direct reports is because you can only care for so many people. Sure, you can manage lots of people, but you can't really know them or invest in them in a personal way. So, how do you care? First of all, you need to know some basic information about them, their family, their children, and maybe even their pets, which they love more than their children sometimes. Note their birthday, wedding anniversary, and work anniversary. I think you should know their favorite hobbies, restaurants, and even snacks.

Years ago, when you needed to know someone's phone number, you picked up a *landline* phone attached to a wall in your house *(yes, these really existed, millennials and Gen Zs) and dialed* "411" to obtain someone's phone number. The operator held that vital information for every phone customer and would give it out for a small charge of fifty cents. Anyone remember that?

I'm a big fan of maintaining such a list for every team member. I call it a "Team 411 List." Instead of phone numbers, however, we include in spreadsheet form all the other vital information everyone should know about everyone on the team.

The Team 411 List

- Family members
- Birthday
- Wedding anniversary
- Work anniversary
- Favorite hobbies
- Favorite restaurant(s)
- Favorite snacks

Once you have this spreadsheet, it is shared with all the members of the team. This way, at any moment in time, you have the power to very specifically bless a member of the team. You can surprise them with their favorite snack and have it sitting on their desk when they come back from lunch on Monday. You can drop a quick note on his/her birthday. You can celebrate a job well done with a gift card to their favorite restaurant. See the power of this?

This may surprise you, but I am not naturally a caring person. I care; it's just never my first inclination. I am more inherently a task-driven person. Who can relate? If so, you will need to systematize care. One of the reasons I created the "411 List" years ago is so that I could equip my assistant to help me with birthdays, anniversaries, and celebrating achievements. I had a deep desire to grow in my ability to consistently demonstrate care for my team. Effective systems strengthen good intentions.

Sometimes my assistant would say, "Shawn, just so you know, Mary (a member of our team) has been working long hours getting _____ (project) done." The next day I am stopping by her office with a gift card to Perry's (her favorite steakhouse) and a note saying, "Mary, I know you have been laying it on the line for this project. I am thankful. We couldn't do it without you. Why don't you knock off at 4:00 p.m. tomorrow, go home and get the kids situated, and then take your husband out to dinner at Perry's on us." Actions like this are worth a million bucks. Literally, in some cases.

> Effective systems strengthen
> good intentions.

CONTENT

As a leader, you should be a reader! A reading leader is a growing leader. You first need to model the way. As a leader, you should be constantly devouring resources. I chose not to further pursue a coaching engagement with a large tech company this past year because one of the partners in the company actually told me: "I really don't think I need a coach, and I'm not even really a reader. I don't have time for it." I viewed that as a leadership indictment. Not reading is not an option as a leader. You're growing, or you're dying; it's that simple.

As a leader, you should be constantly directing yourself and your leaders to resources. I would suggest as a starting point, pick a great book. Let's just say *this* book. Purchase copies for you and your leadership team. Assign a chapter or two a week. Meet together. Meet thirty minutes a week to discuss it. Have each team member come prepared with their top three takeaways and one call to action for their own personal leadership. Sound complicated?

Being too busy to learn and develop your team is a cop-out. Don't be a victim. Take responsibility to lead your team to the next level! Foster an environment where every team member is encouraged to consistently maintain a self-development plan, but don't stop there. Purchase books that you have read and enjoyed, and gift them to your team. Email interesting articles and links to your team. Always be exposing yourself and your team to resources through websites, blogs, articles, or whatever it might be. Don't be afraid of blowing up your team's inboxes with great content.

Offer every team member a leadership development budget they can utilize at their discretion to invest in resources of their own choosing. Pick out some great TED Talks or conference talks, and play them in your team meetings. In your performance and review process, have each team member set personal growth and development goals.

Then hold them accountable through your regular one-on-one meetings with them throughout the year. Resource your team with usable content!

You can inspire your team through various conferences. Conferences inspire people. There's something about being in a big room with lots of other people who share our struggle, while someone cheers us all on to bigger and greater things. I've been leading conferences for years, and almost every week, I meet a leader who made a very specific, scary, courageous decision at one of our conferences. We try to provide that kind of environment at our conferences, but frankly, we are not the only ones. And of course, traveling together with our key team members is half the fun and at least half of the development that happens.

COACHING

I, frankly, have never run across a breakthrough leader or a breakthrough organization who didn't give a mentor or coach a lot of credit for the said breakthrough. Every leader at every layer of our team needs coaching. Every company needs a coach. Every church needs a coach. Every non-profit needs a coach. Every leader needs a coach! You need a coach. I have invested easily six figures and maybe even seven in my own self-leadership over the last twenty-plus years. I tell leaders all the time that if you are ever listening to or reading what I have to say and you think to yourself,

I've heard that somewhere before, I can guarantee you have! I have never had an original thought! Everything I know I learned from someone else somewhere else. I have simply ingested the content, contextualized it, simplified it . . . and made it better!

The same is true for you. Everything you know you learned somewhere else from someone else. So, if you're not in a coaching relationship, and you're not learning, well, you're dying. You will run out of things to say. You will become lax. You will get lazy in some of your habits. Experience alone won't make you better. It's experience followed by feedback.

Most experts and fans agree that retired NFL quarterback Tom Brady was and is the "GOAT" (greatest of all time). Tom threw for nearly eighty-five thousand yards and over six hundred touchdowns in his prolific career while winning seven Super Bowls. Experience? He had it. Tenure? He had it. Over ten thousand hours invested into his craft? Check. However, consider this: even in his final season—after twenty-two years in the NFL—Tom still had a quarterback coach! If anyone ever deserved to say, "You know, I don't think I need a coach anymore," it would be he. Yet, every time he dropped back to pass, he still had a coach watching his every move. "Tom, watch it, you're dropping your elbow." "Tom, we need to work on your slide." "Tom, you missed an open receiver on that play." Tom not only allowed this type of feedback, but he also sought it out. His career stands as a testimony to what determination combined with coachability can accomplish.

On the flip side, I heard Nick Saban, head coach of the Alabama Crimson Tide, once say, "Average talent doesn't want to be coached." Average talent might say, "Why doesn't everyone just leave me alone and let me do my job." Elite talent is always looking over at their coach and asking the question: "What could I do better?"

As the leader, I want to build an environment where coaching is normative. I'm going to debrief every experience. I'm going to debrief every event. I'm going to debrief every encounter I witness with customers or congregants. And when I'm meeting with a team member in my one-on-one meetings, I'm going to say, "Hey, by the way, I want to celebrate. You knocked (this event) out of the park. Hey, I did notice this one thing that I'd love to see you work on. I feel like if this one lagging piece of your leadership was in place, you'd knock it out of the park on a whole new level." As a leader, I am always coaching, and I should always have a coach.

DEVELOPING "FIRST-CLASS" LEADERS

I fly around the country a lot. I speak, write, and consult with leaders all across the globe. When I travel, I don't usually book first-class tickets, but because of my flight status with the various airlines, I am always on the shortlist for complimentary upgrades! If you are familiar with the first-class section of a commercial airline, your flight experience is quite different than everyone else's.

First, you get to board and exit the aircraft before everyone else. When you arrive on board, the seats are larger and recline further, and the rows are wider. There's bottled water waiting at your seat when you arrive there. There's a special flight attendant assigned to your section that waits on you and responds to whatever you need. They take your coat and hang it for you and then return it to you just before you land. There are complimentary earphones and unlimited snacks and drinks. Ready to fly now?

If you've flown first class, do you remember the first time? You didn't know the protocol. You knew you didn't belong up front with all the wealthy people, but you tried to act like you knew what you were doing. You were probably thinking to yourself, *I know I don't belong here, but I need to pretend I do.* You watched and observed. You tried to mimic what the wealthy did. After some observation, you caught on. Now, when I am sitting in first class, I can always pick out the first-class newbies. They look out of place, lost.

Me? It took me a while, but I have finally embraced the fact that I belong. I have literally paid my dues and earned my right to be here. First class is where I belong! Can I let you in on a little secret? You are a first-class leader. There's a reason you sought out this resource. Maybe you bought it, or maybe someone gave it to you because they recognized you as a leader. You have responsibility. You have a team. You have influence. Leadership is influence. That's powerful. That makes you a first-class leader in my book. My challenge to you? Act like it. Act like you belong in first class. Carry yourself as a leader. Wield your influence in a positive manner.

When you start a company, church, nonprofit, or new role, you can be rough around the edges, and the office can look like a frat house in the early days. Your vehicle might look like you live in it, and you can wear a hoodie into the office. However, as your organization and leadership influence grows, you must become more aware of your surroundings. You are increasingly rubbing elbows with a different caliber of clientele. You've been bumped up to first class. You need to start acting like you belong here. What does this look like specifically? Six different characteristics define those who fly at the next level.

Polish

They say a picture is worth a thousand words, so the first snapshot people take of you is really, really important. The Bible tells us that God looks at the heart, but the first part of the verse is the often overlooked: "People look at the outward appearance, but the Lord looks at the heart."[11]

Did you catch that? God looks at the heart, but what do people look at? The "outward appearance." Wow, no truer words have ever been spoken. People judge by appearance, don't they? People tend to make snap judgments. You never get a second chance to make a first impression. People are watching you, surveying you, sizing you up and determining if you are a leader worth following. You are always being interviewed by people. People are asking themselves: *Is this someone worthy of my following them? Is this someone worthy of my trust or investment? Does this person have their life together more than I do?*

The way you carry yourself is a big part of that. I call it polish. Is your life polished: ordered, organized, and neat? Does it look sharp and communicate excellence and first-class leadership?

I generally like to dress just a little sharper and nicer than anyone I am going to meet that day. Why is my dress all that important? First of all, polish communicates *honor* and *priority*. Years ago, most of us got dressed up to go to church. These days in church, anything goes, and there are parts of that I like, but maybe we've lost something along the way.

---

11 1 Samuel 16:7 (NIV)

See, dressing up to go to church was intended to communicate to God and everyone else that God deserves only our best. Our outside appearance was a symbol of our internal desire to bring our best to God. We still dress up to go to weddings and funerals and even into the courthouse when we appear before a judge. Why? Polish communicates honor and priority.

So it is with your team, your customers, and your congregants. Either you look first-class, or you don't. If you think about it, polish also communicates *authority*. I'm a big ESPN fan, and it's interesting to me that on a sports network whose primary audience is overweight, over-the-hill sports jocks, they routinely require their sports analysts to wear suits and ties. Why? Because polish communicates *authority*. Something about seeing someone dressed professionally gives that person more clout in our minds.

Rest assured, *your* sense of polish (or lack thereof) communicates something too. The way you carry yourself communicates honor, priority, and authority, or it doesn't. Am I saying you need to wear a suit or dress everywhere you go? No. Am I saying you should take a bath and iron your clothes? Yes. You can even be casual and still look like a professional. Be polished. Be clean. Be neat. Be sharp!

I also want my car and workspace, our offices and campus, and everything we deliver with our brand to communicate . . . polish! That's first-class leadership.

Poise

I can always pick out the people who have never flown before. They freak out at the first sign of turbulence. Even inexperienced flyers wince and wiggle more. I can also spot new or inexperienced leaders from a long distance away. They freak out at the least sign of organizational turbulence. They lose their minds over a small issue. They allow small bumps to scare them, disturb them, or distract them. First-class leaders maintain their *poise* in the face of turbulence.

The word *poise,* according to Dictionary.com, is defined as: "A dignified, self-confident manner."[12] In short, to have poise means to maintain your composure. Great leaders don't lose their composure easily. You will almost never see a flight attendant lose their poise. They have been there, done that, and gotten the T-shirt. Little surprises them. They are veterans, and their demeanor shows it. They don't flinch during even the most difficult of turbulence.

People who are used to being at this altitude, man, they're not going crazy. Lesson? Don't allow turbulence to cause you to lose your composure. In fact, when turbulence comes along, everyone is watching you. They will follow your cue. Do you think flight attendants ever have moments aboard a plane when they even become fearful? You bet. You just won't know it because flight attendants know that

---

12 "Poise Definition & Meaning," *Dictionary.com*, https://www.dictionary.com/browse/poise.

they set the tone for the rest of the aircraft during times of turbulence. They might be freaking out on the inside, but on the outside? Perfect calm. First-class leaders, you need to learn to do the same. Stay calm. Stay confident. Stay courageous. Say that out loud. I have this written down on an index card on my desk. You should consider doing the same. That way, when you hit a little turbulence, you can quickly glance at it.

Veteran leaders aren't as easily frustrated or agitated. They rarely lose their cool and never freak out. They maintain their dignity, self-assurance, and composure. If crazy is contagious, so is confidence. Keep. Your. Poise.

Promptness

If you think about it, saying you will be somewhere at a certain time and not showing up at that time shows you lack integrity. Saying you are going to start a meeting at 8:00 a.m. and not starting it until 8:20 a.m. because half the team (including myself) were running late begins to set culture. Culture is often created by what we tolerate—in ourselves or in others.

I know this sounds simple, but . . . be on time! Start on time! End on time! If you are the leader, you ought to be the first one to the meeting. You need to be there to greet and fist bump each team member as they arrive. Blowing in at the last moment, looking frazzled, just sends the message that your life and leadership are out of order.

Answer your phone. If you're unable to answer, return your phone calls the same day. Make "inbox zero" a goal for each day or at least every other day. Promptly return emails and texts, too. Be prompt! That's how first-class leaders roll.

Passion

How many of you are smart enough to admit you may not be the sharpest knife in the drawer? That's me, okay? I have boasted over the years about being thirteenth out of my high school graduating class in terms of GPA, but there were only sixty-four of us! That was in Alabama! We are forty-eighth on most national lists. Thank God for Mississippi and Louisiana! I was a B- student in college. I scored a seventy out of a hundred when I originally took the state real estate exam years ago.

> You don't have to be the most brilliant person in the room. You just need to be the most passionate.

And, people do follow me. I have built some killer teams composed of people much more brilliant than I am. The good news for you? You don't have to be the most brilliant person in the room. You just need to be the most passionate.

People follow passion, so you must show up with passion for your team. If you're the most passionate, people smarter than you will actually follow you. You must inspire people. We'll talk in more detail about this later. As for now, bring passion to whatever room you find yourself in.

Positivity

Be a glass-half-full person. Believe in yourself. Believe in people. Believe the best about people. Give them the benefit of the doubt. Don't focus on problems; focus on possibilities. The next time your team hits a roadblock, just step up and say: "Okay, this is not a problem; it's a setback. It's just a challenge and one we're going to overcome. We'll wrestle around with it, until we come up with a solution and a breakthrough."

THREE REASONS PEOPLE LEAVE OUR TEAM

No team member will be with you forever. In fact, many times, there are a couple of people you *wish* would leave. (Yes, I just said that out loud!) The last thing you want to do, however, is lose people that you don't want to lose. We talked about "The Great Resignation" of 2021. The

COVID-19 pandemic, tangled with governmental shifts and decisions, caused a tidal wave of resignations. Organizations of all sizes, in every sector, faced a monumental exodus of talent.

The *Harvard Business Review* cited numerous studies that indicated that over 40 percent of employees across industries were considering quitting their jobs within the next six months.[13] How do leaders and teams retain their best people in the face of tidal waves of resignations? In this section, I want to talk about how you can build a killer team that not only recruits but also *keeps* your best talent.

I was once in a coaching session with a C-suite leader at a multibillion dollar finance company headquartered in New York. Their company had been enjoying quarter after quarter of revenue growth for years. Yet, they seemed to be consistently chewing through talent and experienced more turnover than other companies in the same sector. I was asked if I could think of reasons why.

I responded by saying, "I can probably tell you why they left."

"Okay," she said. "Give it your best shot because I actually conducted exit interviews with many of them."

---

13 Ian Cook, "Who Is Driving the Great Resignation?" *Harvard Business Review*, 15 Sept. 2021, https://hbr.org/2021/09/who-is-driving-the-great-resignation.

I was up to the test. This was not my first rodeo. I told her what I will tell you today. First of all, people don't quit organizations. They quit leaders.

The three main reasons leaders give for quitting leaders are as follows:

1) "The leader doesn't really care about me."
2) "The leader doesn't really know what's going on."
3) "We really don't celebrate wins here."

When I shared this with the C-suite leader that day, she responded by saying, "How did you know that's exactly what I heard from them?" As I said, not my first rodeo.

One of the great values of coaching is that you get to learn from the mistakes of others. You get the opportunity to skip over another leader's pain. Why not learn from another leader's mistakes and avoid the pain they endured to learn it? In this case, you can skip over another leader's pain of consistently losing great talent. Know your team. Know what's going on with them. Know what's going on in their personal and professional lives. Know what's going on with *their* team. Don't push. Lead. Communicate. Collaborate. Coach. Celebrate. If you will, you can not only recruit the best talent, but no one and almost no amount of money will ever be able to recruit them away.

BOLSTERING ACCOUNTABILITY

opefully, by now, you are grasping what it takes to build a killer team without killing yourself or your team. Let's recap.

1) Foster togetherness. You're building more creative, consistent meetings with your team. You are building trust by practicing the last 10 percent in your conversations and maintaining a drama-free culture by leaning into healthy, consistent conflict.

2) Recruit and keep the best talent. You're developing leaders at every level and creating a culture everyone wants to become and stay a part of. You are coaching up new talent every day within your organization.

Step three is next. It's time to bolster accountability on your team. *I know, I know. You* want to hold *your* team more accountable. It's easy to think about what our team members owe us and what we want to hold them accountable for, but what exactly are we accountable for *to* our team?

> You have to be the culture you want to build.

In our coaching with leaders, we talk about the Three Gears of Growth©: culture, team, and systems.

THE GEARS OF GROWTH

I can trace every tension and opportunity in your organization back to one of these three gears. When it comes to "culture," the number one responsibility of a leader is to be the culture you want to build. Leadership is caught more than taught. We reproduce what we are. As the leader, you've got to set the example. You've got to model the way.

You've got to be as good as your word. You must demonstrate character in every meeting and conversation. You must live out the values.

A healthy culture closes the gap between what we say we value and what we really value. If excellence is really important in your organization, the question you've got to ask yourself is, *Are we living our lives with great distinction?* If fun is a core value in your organization, the question we must ask ourselves is, *Am I a fun person?* You need to hold yourself accountable to living, being, and maintaining the culture over time.

At one point, during the height of the COVID-19 pandemic, I had to apologize to my team. "Health" is the first of our core values, and I had fallen off the wagon. My exercise routine had become lax. I decided to fess up. I walked into a team meeting that week and got honest. "Guys, I owe you an apology. I have fallen off the wagon with my exercise these last few weeks. I've not modeled the way when it comes to our values, and I need to set the example for you. We are not going to grow this organization at the expense of our own health. I never want to hold you all accountable for something that I'm not willing to be held accountable for."

Set the example. Practice what you preach. When you blow it, say, "I'm sorry." Be a person of integrity, character, and trustworthiness. Be approachable and willing to be held accountable. Be a person worthy of being followed.

You cannot delegate culture. Be the culture you want to build. Design the culture you want, and protect and preserve it. "Be mean" about it if you have to. Fight for the vision. Culture happens by default or by design. Be it. Design it. The health of your organization's culture has a direct impact on its growth.

BECOMING AN ACTION-ORIENTED TEAM

Once we're willing to make ourselves accountable, we are now ready to hold everyone else accountable. To do this, you will need to build what I call an "Action-Oriented Team."

Does most of what you talk about in your meetings actually get done? Does your team have a propensity to take action? An organization cannot grow faster than the pace at which it makes decisions and acts upon them. To build a killer team, you must build a team with a propensity to take action.

First of all, as stated earlier, you've got to model the way. You must be an action-oriented person. Be a "DWYSYWD" (Do what you say you will do) person. Teach your team to operate the same way. The Bible says, "Let your yes be yes and your no be no. Anything else is from the evil one."[14] Neither you, nor your team members, should need to swear and promise to do what you are going to do. Talk is cheap. You

---

14 Matthew 5:37 (NKJV)

must back it up. Your walk must match your talk. You must follow through. You must be good as your word. You must trust each other to do what you tell each other you are going to do. The road to hell is paved with good intentions. Hope is not a strategy. I can teach you how to build a system for this.

In an environment that's action-oriented, you will be constantly pausing in meetings to say, "So, what are we going to do about it?"

Action-Oriented Meetings

If you want to inspire the best members of your team, create an environment where the things you talk about in meetings actually get done. To do that, make someone responsible in every meeting for taking "action-oriented minutes." The average team takes minutes in meetings: what was discussed, who said it, etc. I don't really care what was discussed or who said it. Your recorded action-oriented minutes will include:

- What did we decide?
- Who is responsible for it?
- When is it due?
- When do we need an update?

In every meeting I lead, someone is responsible for recording the answers to these four questions. If it's not clear, they have permission to interrupt the meeting by saying:

- "Wait, what did we actually decide?"
- "Wait, who is responsible for this?"
- "Wait, when is this due?"
- "Wait, when do we need to talk about this again?"

I want these answers recorded in a document that's placed in the cloud. I want this document accessible to everyone who was in the meeting, as well as those who couldn't make the meeting, so they can stay in the loop.

And then guess where we start the next meeting? We start the next meeting with, "Hey, what did we decide last meeting? Who was responsible for it? When is it due? Let's get an update." Only then, do you begin to build a culture that's action-oriented.

Here's your homework. Visit killerteambook.com and download the free "Action-Oriented Minutes Template" for your team. Implement this process into your meeting framework, and boom—you have bolstered accountability!

CHAPTER
— 9 —
REVIEWING YOUR TEAM

We've been talking about bolstering accountability. One of the best ways to inject more clarity and accountability into your culture is by implementing and maintaining a healthy performance and development review process. If you've been part of a less-than-killer team, they would use a phrase like "staff evaluation."

First, language matters. Second, the goal of this process is not to "evaluate" people. The process is utilized to *review performance* and *develop* members of the team. This is a leadership development tool that provides encouragement, inspiration, and clarity in addition to accountability. You will utilize this to help coach and cultivate everyone on your team. This tool will also be helpful in allowing you to communicate more clearly when team members are not meeting expectations. We owe them the truth about that. This tool and process will also serve to help a few team members self-select and more naturally pull the ripcord themselves when they are no longer a fit on the team.

Let's talk about how to have the conversation. One of the values of coaching is you have a leader holding your hand, helping you do the right thing the right way. One of my fears is that this tool could be used for harm. My fear is that you would adopt part of the process but not all of it. Make sure you use this tool consistently and constructively. I can help you do this if you stay tuned.

The first thing to do is get performance and development reviews on the calendar for everyone. Go ahead. Set the dates. For now, just get the first round on the calendar, and let everyone know this is coming. This is best to do in person—not in a mass email to the team; that way, there's more opportunity to explain the why behind the what.

Second, allow each direct report to take their own copy of the performance and development review, and I want them to review themselves. You heard me. I want them to review themselves first and foremost. The most encouraging thing about this part of the process is that your best talent is going to be harder on themselves than you'll ever have to be. I have found that the best leaders—those I wanted to get and keep around me for a long tenure—were ones who were really hard on themselves, and I actually had to soften the blow. So, allow them to review themselves first, then lead the discussion. Have them come to the table, share their answers to their questions one at a time. Then I give my answer, and we come to an agreement about reality. I want to give every team member an opportunity to "grade" themselves, as I will explain later, and share why they gave themselves the score they did.

The other almost humorous part of this process is that we will always have "that person" (or two) on the team that lacks self-awareness. They are brilliant but lack emotional intelligence. Okay, you have that person in your mind. It never fails. Their cluelessness will come across in the review. They will demonstrate and display their lack of ability to read a room or properly assess themselves. Who gets it? Who realizes they need to improve and are open to it? Who thinks they are fine, and that that's okay? This step in the process can provide some clarity for us from the very beginning!

At the bottom of the review, there's a place to summarize by forming a simple leadership development plan. What now? Where do we go from here? What are my targets? What do we do next? How does that inform our development over the next six months?

THE CONTENT AND GRADING PROCESS

If you ask me, the "grading" system for a healthy performance and review process is foundational to the entire exercise. I advocate using five categories or "buckets" in which every score will lie: exceptional, very good, good, acceptable, and unacceptable. We don't stop there, either. We need to define each of these, so every team member knows what their score(s) mean.

- **Exceptional**: Consistently far exceeded all expectations.
- **Very Good**: Consistently exceeded normal expectations and job requirements.
- **Good**: Consistently met all minimum expectations and job requirements.
- **Acceptable**: Usually met expectations and minimum job requirements.
- **Unacceptable**: Below the bar of minimum expectation.

As you can see by the language used on the scale, there are lots of opportunities to encourage members of our team. If the team member always exceeds all of our expectations, wow, we owe it to them to tell them that! Honestly, though, who *always* exceeds *all* expectations? Very few. That's why I give very few "exceptional"s in my reviews, and I tell my team members that. Once you're exceptional, you can't improve any further! What's the fun in that?

> Once you're exceptional, you can't improve any further! What's the fun in that?

When we get down to good, well, that means . . . good! It's not average. Good really means you are doing everything you are supposed to do and staying out of trouble. Good also communicates room to grow to another level and develop greater killer instincts and habits.

Acceptable means you're doing okay. You usually stay out of trouble. You do enough to get by. You're not flashy. You're not in danger of getting fired. However, I would love to see more. I believe you have more in you. You have potential that you're not tapping into as of yet, and I want to call that out.

Unacceptable means just what it says. The behavior or metric is below the bar of minimum expectation, and I owe it to you to tell you that. If a team member has fallen from acceptable to unacceptable in an area of their behavior or performance, they deserve to know about it sooner rather than later. Usually, I advocate within the system that if you end up with two or more unacceptable areas on your review, we are not going to wait six months to talk about this again.

You have ninety days to bring at least one of these up above the bar into the acceptable category. If you haven't been able to do this in ninety days, the odds are that you are never going to be able to do it, so we need to talk honestly ninety days from now as to whether this position or this team is the best fit for you.

Do you see how clear that is? Do you see how this allows more opportunity for a team member to come to the conclusion themselves that they are in the wrong seat or on the wrong team? Clarity and accountability win every time.

Remember, all of this is a coaching and development tool. The only reason I even care about reviewing your past six months of work is because it allows me to debrief your performance and be your coach. "Hey, you're dropping your shoulder when you throw," or "Hey, you're getting happy

FOCUS ON WHERE YOU WANT TO GO

"EVALUATION"
= LOOKS BACK

"REVIEW &
DEVELOPMENT"
= LOOKS AHEAD

feet in the pocket," (if you don't know what that means, ask a football fan).

I let my team members know before the review that I am going to encourage, but I am also going to be a little hard on them. My job is to care about them enough to not allow them to stay the way they are. They have potential and growth inside of them that they don't even understand, and I want to call it out. I want to squeeze every ounce of potential out of them, and I'm just utilizing this as one tool in the tool belt to do so.

Ninety-nine percent of the time, these reviews are encouraging and inspiring. There's often laughter and sometimes tears, but we are dialoguing at a level in this conversation that we might not ever otherwise obtain. This tool normalizes a coaching environment and provides content and a framework for coaching all of my direct reports over the course of the next few months.

What *exactly* are we reviewing? Stay tuned. I have your answers.

Behaviors

Yes, we are going to set goals in the performance and review process, but we don't need to start there. The first component of a healthy performance and review process is vision, clarity, and alignment. Does this team member really understand the vision? Are they living out the values of the organization? Are they setting a good example? Remember, as an organization, we are now holding ourselves accountable for behaviors that align with our beliefs, so these behaviors (values) need to be identified, articulated, and discussed during a healthy performance and development review process.

Modeling the vision and each of your core values should be outlined in your performance and development review, and every team member should know how they are doing in regards to each of them. We owe them that.

Expectations

The second area of a healthy performance review process has to do with clarity as it relates to job skill, implementation, and expectations. This section would include review of a team member's job description, previous goals, and any areas where a team member has struggled previously.

At the conclusion of this meeting, you will make copies of both versions of the review, and you will hold on to one set of copies and provide one for each team member. Then, one week before the next review, they are emailed a copy of the last review. We are looking for progress. We are looking for growth. We are developing our team, spurring them on, holding them accountable, and releasing the rest. Wow, can you feel it? You are building a killer team . . . without killing yourself or them!

You're not even done! You're going to use this as a coaching tool on a consistent basis. You're going to be offering coaching weekly, if not daily, as a follow-up. You're going to put this on your calendar every six months. I have always liked the first week of May, before everyone goes on summer vacations, and early December, before Christmas, while promotions/raises/bonuses are being considered. Consistently meet with and coach your team members.

But wait, there's more! If this content is important, then it should be important to everyone all the time. So, you are going to pull out this tool, and go over it with prospective team members. Make it part of your hiring process. Talk about your organization's performance and development review process during new employee orientation. You're going to use it as a normal part of your dialogue and coaching in your one-on-one and team meetings.

If you are a really good leader, write team leadership lessons and pen consistent emails that are distributed throughout the organization throughout the year that highlight the behaviors and expectations you aspire to. You're going to publicly embarrass team members who are getting the most "exceptional"s. What gets celebrated eventually gets emulated by everyone. This is how you really begin to drill this down into every layer of your organization.

> What gets celebrated
> eventually gets emulated by
> everyone.

Again, I talk much more about how to drill vision and expectations into every level of the organization in my book *Be Mean About the Vision*. Visit killerteambook.com for discounts on copies of this book for you and your team.

CHAPTER
10

RELEASING SOMEONE THE RIGHT WAY

lite talent can't stand to be around below-average talent. Performers and underperformers are like oil and water: They don't like to mix. Healthy team members can't stand to be around drama. Many times, in our leadership careers, we are going to come to the conclusion that we must make a tough decision with someone on the team. Usually, this person has already begun to stick out like a pink elephant in the room no one wants to talk about. Oh, everyone sees it. They just don't have the authority to do anything about it. You are the leader. You have that power.

Please also hear this: If someone no longer fits or belongs on the team, and you choose to do nothing about it, you begin to lose credibility. The other members of the team begin to wonder if you have the ability to recognize these issues and/or the courage to do anything about them. People are going to leave your team. Performers will leave if underperformers are not being held accountable. Healthy people will leave if

the culture is becoming toxic. Why not release the underper-
former and the toxicity before that happens? The ultimate
accountability arrives when we realize that a candidate can't
and shouldn't go with us further into the future. Once we
have made that determination, much wisdom and courage
are needed to handle this delicate decision the right way.

You need to move them off the team, but how do you
do it? Well, the right timing, tone, and temperature are all
important. Often in leadership, coming to the conclusion
of what needs to be done is only 25 percent of the process.
Understanding how to do the right thing the right way is a
full 75 percent of the process. If we do the right thing the
wrong way, we still blow everyone and everything up. This
is one of the great values of having a coach. A coach helps
people process through all the dynamics and not only do
the right thing but also do it the right way.

In the pages that follow, I want to give you a step-by-
step process for releasing someone . . . the right way.

> If someone no longer fits or
> belongs on the team, and you
> choose to do nothing about it, you
> begin to lose credibility.

DON'T PROCRASTINATE

Once I was taking a tour with a leader of a successful, multimillion dollar campus in Southern California. As we toured, we talked. Their team had just made a difficult choice to release a high-level team member because of some character issues that had bubbled their way to the top. I asked the leader about turnover within his organization, and he stopped. He pointed up at one of the large buildings on campus and said: "See the wing of that building? That's our HR Department. We have hired the people that work there from some of the finest HR firms in the country. We still get hiring right, at best, 50 percent of the time." You probably don't have an entire HR wing at your disposal, so you may have as good as a fifty-fifty shot of getting every hire right.

Honestly, we don't know if someone is going to fit until they have been here for a while. We never know if someone can keep up until they have been here for some time. Their true character is never revealed in a resume or an interview. It comes out in time due to pressure. Unfortunately, over time, in many cases, we are going to come to the conclusion that a team member never did or no longer fits.

To recognize something's not right on the team and not do something about it is just plain sinful. You're not going to hire everybody perfectly, but once you realize it's not right, the longer you try to hold onto them, the more toxic it's going to become.

Allow this truth to haunt you: In all my years of coaching, I have never had a leader say to me, "Shawn, I had that conversation too soon." On the flip side, if I only had a nickel for every leader who has said to me: "Shawn, I waited too long to have the conversation," I would be a very wealthy man. Allowing time to pass will only bring more sleepless nights, more tension, and more drama in the end. As soon as you finish this chapter, put this book down, schedule the meeting, and have the conversation. Release them. Make the decision. Don't procrastinate.

GO PRIVATELY

If you think you could get sued for wrongful termination or falsely accused of sexual assault on the heels of this release, you might want to take someone with you. Otherwise, in almost every case, you are better off not doing this by committee. A team member is almost always going to be less defensive and less aggressive when they don't feel like they're being ganged up on.

By allowing this conversation to happen one-on-one, we are allowing the person we are releasing to maintain more dignity in the process. The process also comes across as more personal and relational when it's person to person. Sure, if you attempt to meet with someone privately and things start to get dramatic, you can call a time-out and bring someone else to the party. First, however, try to keep the conversation private.

AFFIRMATION

Rarely has this team member done *everything* wrong. They said yes to join the team in the first place. That's something. They contributed positively in some way. Mine for this. Accentuate it. Don't belabor all the negatives. Be balanced in your conversation, and thank them for being part of the team for their tenure.

DON'T SPIN IT

This is not the time to spin something, glaze over under-performance, or avoid discussing vision gaps. Don't blame it on the economy or whatever. Don't spin it. Shoot straight with them. Be honest with them. You should be able to say something like: "Hey, you know we've had multiple conversations about this. We've tried. You've tried. I think we both know things aren't necessarily better. We need to agree it's time to make a decision."

BE GENEROUS

Be generous in your compliments, of course, but also be generous and gracious to them in their exit and as generous as possible in your severance agreement with them. Brace yourself. I'm a fan of ninety to 100 days of financial sever-ance. Be *that* liberal with them. And, don't give it all in a lump sum; string it out over the course of time. This allows you to hold them accountable at some level for taking the high road with you.

ACKNOWLEDGE YOUR PAIN

I believe it's great to let the person know, "Hey, I have wres-tled with this, lost sleep over it. This is not easy, but we need to have this conversation. I'd rather not have it, but we need to. It's important." I tell leaders all the time that if these types of conversations become easy for you, you probably need counseling! Acknowledging your pain to a leader with whom you are having a tough conversation allows them to view you as a human being, not a cyborg that's indifferent to humanity and human emotions. Our approach should communicate care and compassion, clarity and resolve.

ESTABLISH HIGH-ROAD/LOW-ROAD SCENARIOS

The high-road scenario goes something like this: "We are going to agree together today that this is the right thing. You will offer your resignation, and I will accept it. This can be viewed as a mutual decision, and we will honor each other publicly and privately during and following your exit. The high-road scenario says: 'We agree that this needs to happen. We'll do it with honor and courtesy.' I'll believe the best and speak the best about you, and you will offer me the same courtesy. I'm going to provide you with a generous severance, and you will exit with dignity. When your next potential employer calls, I will do my very best to accentuate your positives and offer a good reference.

"The low-road scenario is you walk out of the office, slam the door, and begin to stir up drama within the company. You spew venom. You create posts on Facebook that take passive-aggressive jabs at our organization and leadership; therefore, we cut your severance short and refuse to provide a good reference for you." You conclude by saying, "Which road would you like to take?"

PUT EVERYTHING IN WRITING

Put everything in writing. Listen, once you say, "We're going to have to agree to part ways today," they're not hearing most of what you say after that. You must make sure you put everything in writing. I'm a big fan of what I call an "exit agreement." The exit agreement outlines all of the details concerning a team member's exit from the company: timeline, deliverables, promises, benefits, etc. When is their last day? What benefits are you going to provide? How long is the severance? What about unpaid vacation time? I also encourage organizations to include what I call an "honor clause":

It is intended by you and (organization) that this exit be done in a God-honoring way in all regards. By signing below, we mutually agree to honor each other publicly and privately and not to disparage or speak negatively of each other, in any conversation or any written form, including social media. Any language construed to be damaging in nature to (organization) through any of these means, will entitle the organization to cease all compensation and/or benefits due under this agreement.

INCLUDE A COMMUNICATION PLAN

Pay attention. This is perhaps the most commonly overlooked step in the process. I was coaching a leader just recently who had the process blow up on him because the team member left that meeting and began communicating with the wrong people at the wrong time and in the wrong tone. So, we're deciding in this release meeting who's going to tell whom, who's going to tell what, and when we are going to tell it. It needs to be part of the exit agreement.

Perhaps the number one thing that keeps us from having these courageous conversations is we get caught up in how they're going to respond. For some reason, we picture this old episode of the *Jerry Springer Show* where somebody rips off their shirt and throws a chair against the wall. I've never known of a conversation that's gone that badly. If you are going to walk step by step through a healthy process to release someone the right way, I promise you, it won't get too crazy.

> ## Remember: their response is not your responsibility.

At the end of the day, the team member in question decides how they're going to respond. It's their responsibility. Our responsibility is to have the courage to lead and have the conversation. Their response is not our responsibility! We do the right thing the right way. As a leader, we can't get caught up in being a people-pleaser. We live for an audience of one: Almighty God. We seek to honor Him and do what's right in His eyes. We will need to make decisions that are not the easiest or most popular, but they are the right ones. We trust God with the outcome.

MY PROMISE

If you will work this plan step by step (without skipping even one), you can and will release leaders the right way when it is needed. I trust this has been helpful to you, and perhaps you've thought of a team member today with which this needs to happen. This is your call to action. Schedule the conversation. Don't procrastinate!

STRUCTURING FOR GROWTH . . . AND PEACE

f you are going to build a killer team without killing yourself or your team, you need the right structure. To build the killer team you need to build, you will need to pay more attention to your most precious commodity: your *time*. You only have so much time! You will need to become more focused. While you are spread too thin, you are not able to develop your team the way you should. Time is a more precious commodity than money, but we incessantly measure how much money we have in the bank and we manage how we spend it, but very few of us monitor as closely how we manage our *time*.

YOUR MOST PRECIOUS COMMODITY

The most difficult person you will ever lead is yourself. Your life is perfectly structured for the results you are getting now. Your organization is perfectly structured for the results it's getting now. If you want different results in either, the first thing you will probably need to structure is your time. You simply cannot be all things to all people and scale to every edge of your organization.

The scariest truth I will share with you is this: You are probably the most disciplined, prioritized person on the team. I know . . . shocking and scary, encouraging and discouraging at the same time. You need to become more focused and more disciplined, so you can help each member of your team do the same.

What are your priorities? What are the five things you do that, when you do them, provide the greatest potential return on investment for your organization? I call these your Fab Five. We include the Fab Five in our coaching tool called the Five Pillars of Accountability. You can download this worksheet at killerteambook.com.

Just so you know, incessantly checking your email does not belong in your Fab Five, but does it belong on the list? Outlining these five things is going to help you determine how you spend your week. What I love about the Fab Five, is that there are five days of the week. Five (plus or minus) workdays a week give you ample opportunity to calendarize these five priorities. Regardless of your title, position, or career path, I can give you some broad suggestions for how you can and should spend your time each week.

Twenty percent of your time should be spent alone, working on yourself and working on the organization.

This is when you grow. As a leader grows, so grows the organization. This is when you get coaching. This is when you get leadership development. This is when you work on strategy. This is when you work on the future. This is when you dream. This is when you come back to your *why*. Leadership forms best out of the overflow of our own passion and development.

> Twenty percent of your time should be spent alone, working on yourself and on the organization.

One of the few positive things that have come out of the COVID-19 pandemic is that a lot of leaders have realized: *You know what? I don't need to be in the office all the time. In fact, some things run more smoothly when I work from home!* Killer teams experienced an increase in production and innovation during the pandemic, not a decrease. Why? Because they had time to work *on* it, not just *in* it.

Roughly 20 percent of your time should be spent with your team. When I look at your calendar, I should see weekly team meetings and one-on-one meetings with all of your direct reports, as well as strategic huddles for various projects, events, etc. You're not too busy for your team. You're not waiting until things slow down. You're not avoiding your team. You're building a killer team by prioritizing your time with them.

Spend the next 20 percent of your time with your current clients, customers, congregants, donors, etc. The best customers are the ones you have now. Focus on the top 20 percent. Spend consistent time with your largest clients and potential difference-makers. Ask them how it's going. Survey them. Listen to them. Value them. Ask for their opinions and feedback. Prioritize retention. The old adage is true. Twenty percent will make at least 80 percent of the difference.

If you're decent at math, you have 40 percent of your time left to drive growth in your organization. Devote it to leading your organization to the next level. You're prospecting, posting on social media, driving the marketing. I get at least one message a week from someone who's interested in becoming a coach or consultant with us only because they can't make a living coaching on their own. Let me tell you why: They get a few early clients, and then all of their time is absorbed with serving those few clients. They have no strategy to keep the inbound funnel consistent by bringing in new business. New business is critical. Are you following me? Don't wait to see how your week unfolds. Plan your week rather than allowing it to plan you. Initiate, don't react in your leadership. Place your priorities on the calendar as set appointments, and come hell or high water, don't allow anything to get in the way. Make your decisions in advance, and fulfill them daily.

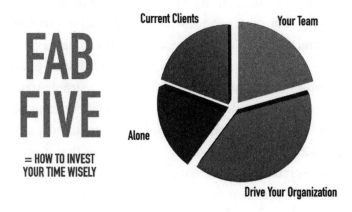

FAB FIVE

= HOW TO INVEST YOUR TIME WISELY

Current Clients · Your Team · Drive Your Organization · Alone

Once again, we offer a simple tool titled "Taming Your Calendar" for you to use in this process at killerteambook.com. It's also a great resource to share with your team to assist them in becoming more focused, prioritized leaders. We don't presume on growth. We get prepared for it.

RESTRUCTURING YOUR TEAM

Are you ready for another dose of what could be a difficult truth? If your smartphone is blowing up, your inbox is filling up, and your text messages are stacking up—and that's just from your team members—you have a problem. Specifically, you have a structure problem. You're either not correctly structured, or you're not operating by the structure you've outlined. The good news, once again, is that you can break this cycle. There is a way to structure for growth and peace. In this section I want to help you do just that.

Sure, Amazon is good at selling things online, but when analyzing the company's success, it goes much deeper than that. Why has Amazon been so wildly successful? If you look closely, elite leadership combined with simple structures and systems can be found everywhere. For example, in the early days of Amazon, Jeff Bezos instituted a rule: every internal team had to be small enough that it could split two pizzas. They called it the "two-pizza rule." My only pushback? I think for most leaders, that's too many people. More people can lead smaller teams.

At Courage to Lead, we advocate leaders build "one-pizza teams." I actually don't want more people reporting to someone than can split a pizza. That's usually four or five (at the most six) people. You can manage seven, ten, twelve, fourteen people, but can you truly care for and develop that many people? Can you meet one-on-one with that many people, review that many people every six months? Can you know your team members' children's names? You should.

If you think about it, larger team dynamics also stifle the best dialogue and collaboration. A couple extroverts will tend to dominate the conversation, and at least two or three (maybe five to seven) people will rarely speak up. The best ideas will never make it into the meeting. The more people on the team, the greater potential for miscommunication and confusion.

This is why you don't want more people reporting to anyone than can split a pizza. That's the limit . . . for everyone, including you. At every organizational level, you're going to enact and enforce the one-pizza rule. At the end of the day, every team member needs to know clearly who they answer to. No one (and I mean no one) should have two bosses.

Part of the beauty of this exercise is being able to articulate more clearly the difference between authority and influence for every team at every level. To structure for growth and peace, no one on your team needs to feel like they have two bosses, like they answer to two people. So, I want to clearly define the authority line—the solid line, I call it—and the influence or dotted line. You owe this level of clarity to your team. Who has authority over certain decisions versus influence in those decisions? Does this person or team inform my decisions or approve them? Go to killerteambook.com to access a one-pizza team organization chart that can provide the clarity your team needs. Once again, we have provided a one-pizza team organization chart template for you and your team over at killerteambook.com.

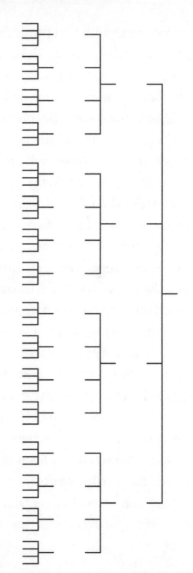

One-Pizza Team Organization Chart

The final thing you want to pay attention to is the ratio between "products" and "projects." I mentioned earlier in the book that experience won't necessarily make people better. Performance followed by feedback lifts people to the next level.

You're often going to hire entry-level positions for your team. The people hired for these positions will often be young, inexperienced, and wet behind the ears. These are the projects on your team, and they're found at the low end of the pay scale. Projects are green; they need a lot of development and work. They need consistent coaching, but they've got a huge upside. They're diamonds in the rough.

Maybe you lead a start-up today, and that's all you can afford. You are the product, the one with experience, the proven commodity, the more seasoned leader. Your responsibility, then, is to help the projects become products over time. Reproduce yourself in your team.

As an organization grows, however, you can't be the only product. You will need more. Every time you add four or five projects, someone will need to step up to be the product over that team, or a product will need to be recruited from outside the organization.

At the top of every team at every level, I need to place a product. It needs to be someone I can pull off the shelf over there and place over here, and they can hit the ground running because this is not their first rodeo. Products are more plug-and-play. They have been there, done that, and they have the leadership scars to prove it. They are first-class leaders, and they act like it. They are poised, polished, and proven. Products lead your projects in the conversation.

If it's just you and a bunch of projects, you will only get so far.

If you are the only product, and you're completely surrounded by projects, then you become the lid; you will only get so far. You need a healthy ratio of projects and products, developers and doers. It's imperative you consistently cultivate the young, inexperienced talent on your team because they won't get better by themselves. Experience won't make them better. On your one-pizza team, place a product over a few projects, and watch them grow, mature, and reach the next level in every stratum of the organization.

If you will work through the filters above as you structure for the future, you will begin to develop leaders at every level in your organization. Don't overcomplicate it. This is your leadership pipeline. You're structuring your team for both health and growth—and peace!

TENDENCIES THAT SABOTAGE OUR TEAM-BUILDING

F rankly, I've never run across a leader that said, "No, I'm not really interested in building a killer team." Everyone likes the idea. The challenge is that too many leaders get in their own way. They give in to natural tendencies that sabotage team-building.

The gravitational pull is away from "we" towards "me." We never wake up one day and say: "You know, I don't want a team," or "Today, I want to disempower my team . . . turn my back on my team . . . blow up my team, etc." Our tendencies that sabotage our team-building are more subtle than that. Let's expose some of the hidden tendencies that can undermine our ability to build the killer team we want to have.

TENDENCY #1: LEADING OTHERS BUT NEGLECTING YOURSELF

The most difficult person you will ever lead is yourself. If you get better, everyone and everything else will get better too. So, leader, you must work on you. King Solomon, in the book of Ecclesiastes in the Bible, shared a nugget of wisdom that many leaders have missed: "If the ax is dull and its edge unsharpened, more strength is needed, but skill will bring success."[15]

King Solomon authored the book of Proverbs. History tells us that he experienced firsthand what it meant to be sharp but become dull. In the early years of his life, Solomon prayed for wisdom, and the Bible tells us that he became the wisest man who ever lived. Tragically, however, he used that wisdom to pursue money, sex, and pleasure. He would later author the book of Lamentations in which he bewailed the lack of power any of those things possess to make a person truly happy. His is a tragic story of a leader who lost his edge. He stopped sharpening the ax. He ceased his daily pursuit of knowledge, understanding, and the will of God for his life. He got lazy, distracted by chasing power, the almighty dollar, pleasure, and too many women. His ax (his wisdom and leadership skills) became dull.

Have you ever chopped wood? I have. I grew up on a farm, and we cut all of our own firewood with a chainsaw. Then, those logs had to be split to fit in our fireplace and burn effectively. I know what it's like to try to chop wood with a dull ax. You have to work much harder and take many

---

15 Ecclesiastes 10:10 (NIV)

more swings to slice through that piece of wood because here's the thing about ax dulling: You can't see it happening. Honestly, from just a few feet away, a dull ax looks the same as a sharp one. The effort the woodchopper has to apply is the greatest revealer of the sharpness of the blade.

> If the ax is dull and its edge unsharpened, more strength is needed, but skill will bring success.
> —Ecclesiastes 10:10 (NIV)

Embedded in this truth is a powerful, encouraging word. You probably don't need to work harder. You simply need to work smarter. In fact, if you are exhausted from your work today, it may simply mean that your ax has gotten dull. You've become lax in your personal development. You've been busy. You've been distracted. You've been pursuing the growth of whatever it is you're building at the expense of staying sharp. You don't have a coach.

Guess what happens when the ax is dull? You work twice as hard to get the result you want. You get tired, frustrated, impatient. You burn out and might even be tempted to give up on the job because even though you've been chopping like crazy, you have a hard time seeing the difference you are making. What is the answer? Stop working for a moment, and sharpen the blade.

Sharpening the blade can mean:

- Hiring a coach.
- Reading a book.
- Listening to a podcast. (I'm partial to the Courage to Lead podcast.)
- Attending a conference.
- Recruiting some new labor.
- Getting some training.
- Training someone else on the team to chop wood.
- Getting the proper physical exercise.

Whatever it looks like, you must sharpen the ax.

THE MYTH OF THE OPEN-DOOR POLICY

Whoever invented the open-door policy was not a leader. You know the policy. You may believe in it and teach it, but it's a very bad idea, and I will prove it. The open-door policy suggests that the leader's door is always open to everyone on the team. The leader is always available to everyone. However, the best gift you give to your team is not your availability or accessibility. The best gift you give your team is a sharpened version of yourself.

One of the greatest tendencies you will have as a leader is to manage everyone else at the expense of managing yourself. Yes, there need to be times when you open the door and make yourself available, but there also need to be times when you are unavailable and inaccessible, so you can be alone, quiet, and work on yourself. You need time to work *on* the business, not just *in* the business. The most powerful tool you have to offer your organization is your own self-leadership time.

The most powerful tool you have to offer your organization is your own self-leadership time.

You may have a plan to grow your company or your church, but do you have a plan to grow yourself? Do you have a strategy to lead yourself to the next level? You must work on you. You must get better. If you get better, I promise you, everyone and everything else will get better. One of our coaches can help you build a plan and then hold you accountable to it. Let's jump on a call and talk about it at couragetolead.com/strategy.

TENDENCY #2: MANAGING INSTEAD OF LEADING

Show of hands. Who likes to be managed? I've traveled around the world asking that question, and I have yet to have someone raise their hand. No one wants to be managed; they want to be led. They also want to be communicated with and inspired. They want someone to invest in them and show them how their role fits into the big picture and how they're making a difference. Thus—the purpose of leadership. Management sucks the life out of the room. Leadership breathes life back into it.

I will let you in on a little secret. When someone sees your caller ID come up on their phone, your email pop into their inbox, or they see you coming down the hallway toward them, they have one of two private thoughts: *Oh, hey, it's Shawn!* or *Oh, hell, it's Shawn!* Of course, they don't say that out loud; they would get fired. They just think it. Their private thoughts reflect what you are to them: A life-sucking leader or a life-giving leader. I want you to be the latter.

Be honest about something: We want everyone to go to heaven, but there are some people we would not want to live on our street when we get there? Don't be pious. These are the people that, if you see them in the grocery store before they see you, you duck into the greeting card aisle. By the way, if you can't think of a person, you might be that person!

What do all the people we tend to want to avoid have in common? They are negative, self-absorbed people. They want to tell you how busy they are by reciting and recounting it all, and I do mean all. They want to tell you their problems and the world's problems. They give you all of the bad news.

The sad truth is that too many leaders will walk into conference rooms this week and begin with statements like:

"Alright, let's get started. I don't really have time for this, but I guess we need to meet."

- "We've got lots of problems to talk about today."
- "We've got some issues I want to address today."
- "What's on fire? What's burning down?"
- "Sorry, I'm late, I've been _____ (self-absorbed recitation to follow)."
- "Hey, do we really need to meet this week? I don't know of any huge problems."

The reason most people hate meetings is because they've been exposed to a bad model. They were never taught to lead life-giving meetings. Life-giving meetings require intentionality, planning, and thought.

TENDENCY #3: BEING TOO BUSY TO MEET WITH YOUR TEAM

If you're too busy to meet with your team, you don't deserve one. The whole idea of team is that we work together. If you can't do that, your priorities are out of balance, your life is disordered, and you may be unworthy of being followed. Your team needs to be encouraged, inspired. They need to be communicated with, have their questions answered and their input heard. They need to be held accountable. None of this can happen if you don't make the time to meet with them!

> Being too busy to meet with
> your team is an abdication of your
> fundamental responsibility as a
> leader.

Being too busy to meet with your team is an abdication of your fundamental responsibility as a leader. If this describes you, you need to apologize to your team. Take your calendar, and prioritize spending more time with the difference-makers close to you.

One of the biggest lies from hell I ever believed was: "When we get to *here* (wherever that is), things will be easier." The truth is that as the organization grows, so grows the complexity. This won't get easier with more nickels and noses. Things become more difficult! If we can't manage things now, we have little hope of doing so later. We must get better . . . now.

The second biggest lie from hell I ever believed was: "When things slow down . . . we will _____ (insert what's important)." The truth? Things never slow down. During the pandemic, the world shut down. We couldn't go to the office or even out to eat, but in the process, things actually sped up! If you're waiting until the pace of life slows down to spend more time with your team, stop. Take responsibility. Take control of your day. The first things that should go on your calendar and in this order are:

- Alone time and away time (including vacation).
- Exercise.
- Date night.
- Family night.
- Team meetings.
- One-on-one meetings with all direct reports.
- Everything else after that.

TENDENCY #4: DELEGATING RATHER THAN EQUIPPING

I'm an anti-delegation coach. I don't want you to delegate. Delegating is dumping. Equipping takes more time and effort. You need to take the time on the front end to allow people to watch you do what it is you want them to learn to do. Let them do it along with you for a season. Watch them do it, and offer feedback before turning them loose. If not, at each level of delegation in your organization, the excellence is going to leak right out of your organization.

INSPIRING YOUR TEAM

Here's a new confession for you that may or may not surprise you. When I spoke about cheering on the team earlier in the book, I failed to mention that I actually was a cheerleader in college. Yes, it's true! I grew up playing football throughout high school but wasn't really good enough to make the field in college, and I missed being on the field. Basically, on a dare, I decided to go out for cheerleading, and I made the team! I spent two years on the sidelines cheering on the Bulldogs of Samford University in Birmingham, Alabama.

I only learned one lifelong lesson while I was a cheerleader: no one needs you when the team is winning with little effort. Many times I felt like the football coaches and players had forgotten us or even looked down on us as cheerleaders on the sidelines. While the team was winning, we were almost considered a nuisance. Everything changed, however, when the team got down. When the clock was running out, and we were three points behind with possession of the football, all of a sudden, every football player looked over at us, waving their arms up and down like air traffic controllers.

They needed us. They were bruised and exhausted but needed to summon the emotional and physical stamina to give it everything they had with the game on the line. They needed to know that we were behind them; we had not given up. They needed us to instill new energy into the stands and onto the field. They needed to know that we believed they could still win! "Home field advantage" is very real. The greater the cheers from the stands, the greater the chance your team has to win.

As I stated earlier in the book, your team doesn't want to be managed, but they do want to be led. It may not be apparent when the team is winning easily. However, when deadlines loom and the team is tired and bruised, they need leadership and inspiration. Even killer teams need to be inspired by their leader!

REMEMBER WHY

I say in my book *Be Mean About the Vision* that if we forget why we're doing what we're doing, we'll eventually lose our passion. When vision leaks, it's like that helium latex balloon you brought home from the birthday party when you were a kid. You fell asleep looking at the prized possession only to wake up the next morning and realize all the helium (the energy) had leaked out! It happened slowly and subtly, and no one really noticed it, but it happened.

It happens the same way on our teams. Vision leaks. You can't see it, but the energy is diminishing every second. We go out and invigorate the team only to turn around a few weeks later to find that the energy we infused has leaked out again. We will need to pump up the team over and over again. Let's be honest. No matter what we do for a living, 95 percent of it is not sexy. Our work life is composed of documents, spreadsheets, phone calls, emails, and meetings with mostly unhappy people.

Are you depressed yet? What keeps everyone inspired? It's not what we do but why we do it. Why are you doing what you're doing? To be rich? Money won't cure misery. To be famous? Fame won't cure wretchedness. We need only look to the lives of the Hollywood elite for proof. So, really, why do you do what you do? I pray it's because you feel called. You are on a mission, living for a cause, and want to make a difference in the world. Do you have a vision for your life and for your team? What is it? The book of Proverbs tells us that "Where there is no vision, the people perish."[16]

---

16 Proverbs 29:18 (KJV)

> Where there is no vision, the
> people perish.
> —Proverbs 29:18 (KJV)

Where there is a lack of vision, things and people die. Churches die. Companies die. Teams die. Plans and strategies die. Passion wanes. Numbness by frequency sets in. We settle for going through the motions and living for the weekends. This is the American way.

Wow, I want so much more for you than that. I want your why to drive your what. I want your life to be marked by passion. Once again, I speak so much more about this in my book *Be Mean About the Vision*.

If you are a leader who's at least gotten to the second or third rung on the ladder toward success, the most important thing for you to manage is your emotional fortitude. If you are overextended, overcommitted, frustrated, and fatigued, it's going to show up on your team. You will tend to forget why.

You will need to consistently come back and remind yourself why you are doing what you are doing. My personal mission is helping leaders and their teams grow healthier and grow faster. I love coaching leaders through what's keeping them awake at night, so they and their teams can lie down and sleep in peace. I live to help leaders break the cycle of overthinking and overanalyzing everything. I love giving leaders permission to have that conversation and make that decision. I love instilling courage and wisdom into a leader and their team.

Man, I love it. This is my *why*. This is what moves me to get up at 4 a.m. like I did today, with a looming book manuscript deadline, and crank out these vulnerable words from me to you. My *why* drives my *what*. So will yours. My challenge to you? Come back to *why*.

REMIND THEM WHY

After you have rediscovered why, you must consistently remind your team why they are doing what they are doing. Celebrate progress. Celebrate wins. Show the connection between their position on the team and the collective win. Talk about the vision. Celebrate the vision. Tell stories of life change and/or customer impact.

If you are not naturally a cheerleader, and you tend to underestimate the importance of this, systematize it. Build inspiration into your meeting rhythm structure. Don't allow a meeting to pass without inspiration. Cheer on your team.

BRING THE ENERGY

Every leader is either a thermometer or a thermostat. A thermometer simply reflects the temperature in the room. It's easy to be a thermometer. Leaders of killer teams, however, are determined to be thermostats. Thermostats set the temperature in the room; they bring the energy. They sit up on the edge of their seat, speak with conviction and passion, and foster a sense of urgency. They tell stories and remind their teams why they're doing what they're doing. As my friend Jon Gordon says in his best-selling book *The Energy Bus*, no one likes to be around an "energy vampire." Energy vampires suck the energy out of the room. Leaders of killer teams bring the energy to the room and protect the energy in the room!

SURROUND YOURSELF WITH INSPIRATION

Who believes in you? I mean, who really knows you, believes in you, and actually tells you as much. If we are honest, most of us cannot build a long mental list. We are going to experience setbacks and speed bumps. We are going to lose a game now and again. We will get discouraged and might even be tempted to give up.

We need to pursue life-giving relationships and find ways to surround ourselves with inspiration. On my desk right now, is a Post-it Note that simply reads "831." Every time I look down and see that Post-it Note, I am reminded of Romans 8:31 (NIV) which says, "If God is for us, who can be against us?" When I get up in the morning and enter our master bath, there's another Post-It Note that reads "Love my dad" from my middle daughter, Madison. When I open my iPhone, there's a picture of my new granddaughter plastered right there in front of me. When I look down at my left hand, there's a golden band there to remind me that I married over my head.

I need to be inspired, to grow, and to learn. I need to go to conferences and listen to podcasts. I need coaching in my life because it inspires me and keeps me from quitting. It gives me permission. I surround myself with inspiration. I need it! You do, as well.

HAVE SOME FUN

If you want your work environment to be a fun place, you have to be a fun person! As the leader, your team tends to think you eat nails for breakfast and don't need to sleep at night. Come on! Be human. Don't be such a prune. Lighten up! Make light of yourself. Plan and systematize some fun things to do throughout the year with your team, from Top Golf to retreats.

Think through when and where your team will probably need to be inspired throughout the year. Don't put all your eggs in one basket (one event). Remember vision will leak—about every six weeks—so put several environments and/or events together throughout the year that will instill new energy and, yes, even fun into your team.

One of the best things you can do to retain your great leaders is have some fun together. They love seeing you in that environment. Be more spontaneous. Walk into a meeting one day and say, "Hey, everybody, get up, hop in your cars. We're all going to Starbucks. Line up; I'm paying for it." Or surprise them with Starbucks or whatever it looks like for you. Watch the energy return to the team.

Smile

Go ahead; pull out your smartphone, and open the camera app. Smile. Then, stop smiling. Which one is more attractive? You got it. Honestly, God made us all more attractive when we smile! Try this on at work. Walk into the office and make eye contact with someone. Don't say a thing; just smile. What happens? Yep, it's extremely contagious.

You're more pleasant and approachable when you smile. You bring life when you smile. You make a decision . . . to smile! Catch yourself more often. Practice this. Stop by the restroom on your way to the next meeting. Look dead in the mirror and smile. Keep it plastered on your face as you walk into that meeting. Watch everything change. You just inspired people. See? This isn't all that difficult.

14

MAINTAINING RHYTHM AND FINISH LINE

promised you I would teach you how to build a killer team without killing yourself or your team. We've done that by helping you foster togetherness, and if you've started executing the plan, you've begun to build more consistent, creative meetings.

We've helped you begin to think about getting and keeping the right talent on your team in the right places.

We've talked about increased the level of accountability and honesty on your team by creating a system that will build and maintain a drama-free culture that balances grace and truth.

We've talked about structuring your organization for growth . . . and peace.

If you've followed through, you now have a healthier organization.

Remember: You can't presume growth. You prepare for it. That's what you've been doing by getting healthier.

This chapter puts an exclamation point on that truth. If you want to build a killer team without killing yourself or your team, the number one thing I want for you at the end of all of this is to be able to finish well as a leader. Stay sane, centered, and married while you're building whatever it is you're building.

How do leaders and organizations fail? I know this: It's not because of the competition. It's not because of the company, church, or cult down the street. It's not because of the government. It's not because of a pandemic. It's not because of a recession.

> Leaders and organizations succeed or crumble from the inside out.

Leaders and organizations succeed or crumble from the inside out. I've had many friends and a few coaching clients who've fallen from the top. They got tired, distracted. They compromised and disqualified themselves from leadership.

My favorite leader of all time once said: "What good is it for someone to gain the whole world, yet forfeit their soul?"[17]

What if you lose your marriage and children, the respect of your team, your friends and partnerships, your joy and sense of fulfillment—your way and your WHY? Don't let this be your story. Healthy leaders build healthy organizations. Unhealthy leaders, well, they don't. And, I don't just mean physical health, even though I do mean that. I'm also talking about emotional health, relational health, and spiritual health.

Run the right race at the right pace. I'm not going to tell you that you need to lead a more balanced life. I actually don't believe in balance. It's neither biblical nor beneficial. I also don't believe it's possible—giving equal time and energy to everything. All of the weights need to be held in balance 24/7, 365. Have you ever met anyone that does that? I haven't. It's not possible; that's why. And the longer you chase this myth, the more condemning it becomes. So, today is the day you declare death to your pursuit of balance. Just say out loud right now: "I quit. No more."

Instead, decide to pursue a life of rhythm. Rhythm is God's idea and God's way. Therefore, it is the more biblical and beneficial way to live.

---

17 Jesus of Nazareth, Mark 8:36 (NIV)

Balance is a myth, a man-made idea. This is why, in today's world, most of us feel guilty when we're at work because we think we should be at home. We feel guilty when we're at home because we think we should be at work. We feel guilty when we're on vacation. We feel guilty when we aren't.

Don't you see there's something wrong with all this? Here's proof: If you think about it, we invented the forty-hour workweek. From the beginning, back in biblical days, people worked from sunup to sundown, twelve hours a day. When the sun went down, they didn't have Netflix (or electricity for that matter), so they went to bed. People got up at daylight and immediately went out into the fields to work . . . twelve more hours. They maintained this pace for six days every week. If you're good at math, that's a weighty seventy-two-hour workweek.

Then the Sabbath came. The Hebrew root word for Sabbath means "to cease." Hebrews understood that one day each week they were to cease work altogether and rest. They were so serious about not working on the Sabbath that they would even prepare their meals the day before, so they maintained a daily finish line for work. For thousands of years, God's chosen people maintained this life of rhythm. Each day they would work twelve hours and relax for twelve hours. Each day maintained a start line and a finish line.

People worked intensely for six days at this pace, and then the Sabbath was the weekly finish line.

> A life in rhythm is maintaining an ebb and flow of intensity followed by rest.

This is what it means to live life in rhythm. A life in rhythm is maintaining an ebb and flow of intensity followed by rest. I speak so much more about the power of living life in rhythm in my book *Measuring Success: Your Path to Significance and Satisfaction* (available on Amazon or at a special rate at killerteambook.com).

Jewish law still maintains this command. For orthodox Jews, even building a fire on the Sabbath is prohibited today. Two thousand years ago, Christians moved their "Sabbath" to Sunday, the first day of the week, to commemorate the day when Jesus rose from the dead.

This tradition has continued throughout history. Many professional offices, as well as restaurants and retail places (most notably Chick-fil-A and Hobby Lobby) continue to be closed on Sundays. However, this tradition is dying . . . in some part because churchgoers want to go out to eat and then go shopping *after church*!

In my book *Measuring Success*, I define success this way: *Success is being loved and respected by those closest to us. Success is being fully where our feet are.* Do you see the correlation? Is it clicking with you? Our pursuit of success has everything to do with living life in rhythm. When you work, you should be fully where your feet are. You shouldn't feel guilty about getting up each day ready to work. In fact, we were made to work.

Further, when we work, we should be fully present. We should be fully engaged in our work. We should bring our very best for the glory of God and to honor God regardless of what we do. The apostle Paul penned these words to the Christians at Colossae two thousand years ago: "And whatever you do, whether in word or deed, do it all in the name of the Lord Jesus, giving thanks to God the Father through him."[18]

Whatever you do and whatever you lead, you should do it with excellence and gratitude. Your attitude and work ethic are to be admired by every member of your team. This is true *for* every member of our team. You all commit to bring your best attitude and your best work ethic to work every day.

---

18 Colossians 3:17 (NIV)

Killer teams don't whine. Killer teams don't complain. Killer teams don't *have* to work. They *get* to work. Years ago, when I was a megachurch pastor, we hung a sign backstage in clear view. I saw it just before I went on-stage to teach the thousands of people who would gather. The sign read: "Thank you God for choosing me. It is a *privilege* to be on this stage."

I handed off that church to pursue an even greater impact, and God has fulfilled His promise for me. In the last few years, I have spoken on dozens of stages all over the world as well as in boardrooms, conference centers, retreats, and coffee shops. The world is my stage. The world is your stage.

What you've chosen to do for a living is inconsequential. What really matters is that you bring your best—all the intensity that you have. You count it a privilege. You take the stage of life each day with excellence of attitude and ethic. You give it all you've got. You leave it all on the stage. Leave it all on the field. You should be exhausted at the end of every day and at the end of every week. Every member of your team should be willing to do the same.

Then you rest. Every day you need a finish line. You need definite time each day when you stop working, you rest, and you become fully present with your family. Remember that part of being successful in life is being fully where your feet are. This includes home. For example, I made a commitment to my wife twenty years ago that I wouldn't walk in the door at the end of the day still on my phone. Sometimes I have to circle through the subdivision a couple of times or sit idling in the car in the garage. When I get home, however, I am home. No laptop at night for me.

> Part of being successful in life is being fully where your feet are.

I maintain a finish line for work each day. Once I go home, I'm home. I remove the CEO and coach hat, and I am focused on being a husband and dad. I also made commitments to my family years ago that I was not going to be out more than two nights a week traveling or otherwise. I am going to have a date night with my spouse every week. I am going to have a day devoted to my kids. These are promises I made to God and my family, and I communicated them to my team.

I don't just want to be healthy and maintain healthy relationships. I want this for every member of my team. At Courage to Lead, our number one core value is "health." I want to set the pace, be the example, and in doing so, maintain the moral authority to do the same with my team.

I make these decisions in advance. I'm not waiting until I have time to get everything done, until things slow down. When does that ever happen? I made this decision a long time ago. I just manage it daily.

I continue this daily rhythm between intensity and rest for, in my case, five days. And then, weekly, I maintain a finish line. I have downtime every single week. This is not only true for me but every member of the team.

You need to learn to live in this rhythm between intensity and rest, and you need to commit to a daily and a weekly finish line. Then, each year, use all of your vacation time. You heard me. Take all of it, and enjoy it! Rest. Play. Have fun. Make memories. Don't open your email or answer your phone. Build this mentality into the framework of your team.

You won't lose capacity; you will increase it! Scientists and psychologists agree that the problem-solving, tactical part of our brain depletes in energy at a slower pace than the creative, innovative side of our brain. Sure, you can solve problems for a much lengthier amount of time, but the innovative, creative part of your brain shut off hours ago. By overworking, you and your team are literally robbing yourselves of your most innovative, creative capacity!

Today, why not make the commitment to pursue success God's way: a life lived in rhythm. Work hard and rest hard. Maintain boundaries for yourself and your team.

Begin to hold *yourself* accountable to living this way, so you can hold your team to the same standard. *This is the secret to building a killer team without killing your team.*

THE BEST GIFT YOU CAN GIVE YOUR TEAM

What is the best gift you think you could give your team? A bonus? A raise? A promotion? Public praise? A private compliment? A Hickory Farms gift basket? The best gift you can give your team is a healthy growing you. They need to know you are working on becoming the best version of yourself. What is your plan? As I have stated throughout this book, hope is not a strategy. Those times when you are unavailable, they won't mind it if they know you are working on you. You need to be away. You need to close the door. You need to be unavailable. You need to be learning. You need to be reading. You need to be growing. You need to be working on the future.

Maintain Upstream Relationships

There are three kinds of relationships in our lives. First, there are downstream relationships. Those are the relationships that are under our authority, or under our influence because we are further along the leadership journey than they are. You should always be investing into a few projects to help them become products.

Second, there are midstream relationships: your peers, your buddies, and your friends. Your team is counting on you maintaining a few healthy friendships with people who understand you, know you, and will hold you accountable to remain healthy and growing.

Third, however, you can't overlook the importance of maintaining upstream relationships. You need to walk with the wise. If you walk with the wise, you will become wiser. You need to mine and search for relationships with people who have built something bigger than you have. You need to fight to get in rooms with people who think bigger than you do. These are generally people who are a little older than and more experienced than you. Every leader needs a coach!

The reason why success can become your biggest enemy is because you begin to think you don't need to learn from anyone else. I have observed this dynamic at work so many times over the course of my coaching career. When an organization achieves a certain level of success, the leader often begins to teach all that they know to other people, at the expense of staying sharp themselves. Don't ever allow this to become your story.

You've had an opportunity while reading this book to be introduced to the value of a simple conversation with a coach. I pray that it's been valuable to you. I pray that it's the beginning of a great relationship, not the end.

Make no mistake; we would love to be your coach during the upcoming season of your leadership and organization. We would love to walk alongside you in the coming days. Even if it's not with us at Courage to Lead, fight to be involved in a coaching, mentoring relationship. Maintain those upstream relationships. Stay sharp, accountable, inspired, and encouraged. If you stop learning, you'll stop growing. If you stop growing, your team and your organization will stop growing. I don't want this to happen to you. I don't want your endeavor to build a killer team to kill you.

> A healthy growing you is your call to action.

"The best gift you can give your team is a healthy growing you" is your call to action. Get a plan. Get intentional. Pull the trigger. We, of course, would love to speak with you about this. Let's jump on a strategy session video call and talk about what coaching could look like for you and your team. Interested? Visit killerteambook.com.

BUILDING A TEAM THAT THRIVES

I promised you that I would teach you how to foster togetherness, get and keep great talent, bolster accountability, structure for growth and peace, and maintain rhythm and finish lines. I believe I've been true to what I promised. You are approaching the finish line of this book and perhaps the starting line for you to build a killer team without killing yourself or your team.

I believe the team God has surrounded you with is a sacred trust. It's a hallowed responsibility that God's gifted you with. You've been blessed to be a blessing. On a weekly basis, look for ways to bless your team. Discover ways to be generous to them. Give back to them. Serve them. Spend time with them. They want to know you . . . the real you. Be transparent and vulnerable with them. Let them see you bleed. Laugh, cry, and empathize with them. Add value to them. Develop them. Coach and challenge them. Spur them on. Catch them doing what's right. Let them know when they are wrong. Share your successes. Celebrate the wins. Applaud progress.

At the end of the day, God is going to hold you accountable for the way you have led, for the people that He entrusted to you. You are not responsible for what or whom you don't have and what you can't do. You are 100 percent responsible for whom and what you do have. This is your stewardship, your responsibility. If you are not responsible with it, why would God trust you with more? If you are faithful, perhaps you will be entrusted with more.

My desire for you is that when you stand before God one day, and He examines the teams you have led and the way you have led them, that He says, "Well done."

You've probably been convicted at times as you have read through this work. That's okay. God's mercies are new every day. If you've made mistakes, own them. You'll get credibility by doing so. Say, "I'm sorry," and move forward.

Commit to get better. Go ahead. Grab a cup of coffee. Sit down right now. Pull out your journal, tablet, or laptop. Begin to formulate a plan to build a killer team . . . without killing yourself or your team.

Greatness never happens by mistake. This includes you and the ones around you. Finish well, and take them with you. Help them cross the finish line with you. That's really the purpose of building a killer team.

Remember, you will need help, hit speed bumps, and experience setbacks. More blessing will bring more complexity. You will need perspective, permission, and accountability. We would love to help you and your team get to the next level and cross the finish line together. Drop us a line at killerteambook.com.

I would love to hear your feedback, pushback, or comments. If God has used this resource in your life and/or the life of your team, drop me an email. If you made it all the way to the end, here's my personal email: shawn@courage-tolead.com. It comes straight to me. I read all of my emails, especially encouraging ones! I would love to hear about the action steps you've taken and the victories you want to celebrate with someone. How has this impacted your life and your team? I would love to hear that.

It's been my honor and privilege to serve you. I will leave you with this quote from Mother Teresa: "Yesterday is gone, tomorrow has not yet come. We have only today. Let us begin."[19] I pray you will do just that. I look forward to hearing from you and seeing you down the road.

Your friend and coach,
Shawn Lovejoy

> "Yesterday is gone, tomorrow has not yet come. We have only today. Let us begin." —Mother Teresa

---

19 Mother Teresa, "Yesterday Is Gone. Tomorrow Has Not Yet Come. We Have Only Today," *Project Finding Calcutta*, https://www.projectfindingcalcutta.com/let-us-begin/.

WE WOULD LOVE...

Ministry leaders and marketplace leaders face unique challenges — and different opportunities. CourageousPastors.com and CourageToLead.com provide coaching specific to your niche, applying our Gears of Growth framework— and more— to your specific context.

WE (REALLY) COACH THE CHURCH.

CourageousPastors.com/strategy

COURAGEOUSPASTORS.COM

...TO BE YOUR COACH!

The leaders certified through our network aren't only coaches, they're former clients and current practitioners. When you speak with a coach, you interact with someone who not only understands the theory of running a thriving organization, you're working with someone who's actively doing it!

CourageToLead.com/strategy

 COURAGETOLEAD.com

ADDITIONAL RESOURCES

COURAGETOLEAD.COM/

INSPIRE

IMPACT CULTURE. INFLUENCE CHANGE

INTRODUCING THE INSPIRE COLLECTIVE

While many churches are effective in equipping Christians for ministry within their walls, some struggle to prepare them for service in other arenas—their workplace, their neighborhood, their social community.

But the call to be change-makers is for all believers: Artists, business people, civic servants, community leaders, educators, mechanics, stay-at-home parents, students, and wait-staff.

That's why the Inspire Collective was established, to help raise up true influencers who are kingdom-focused Monday through Saturday, not just on Sundays.

The Inspire Collective delivers a unique blend of inspiration and application, spiritual and practical, for those wanting to impact and influence their everyday world for Christ.

THE INSPIRE COLLECTIVE OFFERS

- MAGAZINE
- BOOKS
- STUDY RESOURCES
- COURSES
- LIVE CLASSES
- EVENTS
- LOCAL NETWORKS

FOUNDED BY
Mike Kai, Martijn van Tilborgh, Sam Chand

YOU HAVE A MESSAGE THAT NEEDS TO BE HEARD

It's time to innovate the way we package our message and bring it to market!

"If I had Martijn in my life in my earlier years, my impact could have been greater. He has made my world larger and he can do the same for you."

-Sam Chand